Everyday Readers

Everyday Readers
Reading and Popular Culture

Ian Collinson

LONDON   OAKVILLE

Published by

UK: Equinox Publishing Ltd., Unit 6, The Village, 101 Amies St., London SW11 2JW
USA: DBBC, 28 Main Street, Oakville, CT 06779

www.equinoxpub.com

First published 2009

British Library Cataloguing-in-Publication Data

A catalogue record for this book is available from the British Library.

ISBN   978 1 84553 355 7   (hardback)
         978 1 84553 356 4   (paperback)

Library of Congress Cataloguing-in-Publication Data

Collinson, Ian.
Everyday readers : reading and popular culture / Ian Collinson.
    p. cm.
Includes bibliographical references and index.
ISBN 978-1-84553-355-7 — ISBN 978-1-84553-356-4 (pbk.) 1. College
readers. 2. Readers—Culture. I. Title. PE1417.C63723 2009
418—dc22
                        2008032516

Typeset by S.J.I. Services, New Delhi
Printed and bound in Great Britain by Lightning Source UK Ltd, Milton Keynes

Contents

For Bruce

Acknowledgements

Although this book is a monograph it is, like all books, the result of many questions and encounters with colleagues, students and friends. To acknowledge this fact I'd like to begin by thanking the everyday readers who made this book possible by sharing their lives with a stranger. Thanks to Dr Mark Evans who, after encouraging me to publish my research and finding a publisher, then proceeded to keep the project on track, reading a number drafts along the way. Likewise, I am forever indebted to Professor Bruce Johnson (teacher, mentor, colleague and friend) who has guided my work in the right direction for the last 15 years. He will be relieved to know that he can stop asking me 'what about the book?'. I'd like to express my gratitude to Janet Joyce at Equinox for her patience, and thanks to Michael Couani, Tracey-Lee Downey, Dr Sacha Davis, Dr Dominic Fitzsimmons, Liz Giuffre, Professor Tony Mitchell, Dr John Scannell, Sue Starfield, Warwick Shapcott, Becky Shepherd, and James Squire for their material, intellectual, and emotional first-aid during my struggles with the manuscript, of which there were many. To Ann, Stuart, Sam and Isabelle Collinson, at home in the garden of England and my grandmother Marj in London, thank you for the support from a distance, and finally, thanks to Rachel and Tom whose love has freed my mind to better think and write.

Introduction: 'Sinking Signifiers' – Making Books Mean

I rejoice to concur with the common reader; for by the common sense of readers, uncorrupted by literary prejudices, after all the refinements of subtlety and the dogmatism of learning, must be finally decided all claim to poetical honours

Samuel Johnson *Life of Gray*

It is the reader who plays God

Steven Roger Fischer *A History of Reading*

On the hard ground beside the soup vans, scattered like confetti, copies of well-thumbed bestsellers (le Carré, Ludlum, Clancy and King), indicate the presence of the Footpath Library, a Sydney charity that distributes books to the city's destitute. Its founder, Sarah Garnett, started the Benjamin Andrew Footpath Library in 2003 after deciding that she would 'feed the minds as well as the bodies' of the homeless, the hostel residents and the poor of the inner city (cited in Morgan 2007: electronic source). The library gives away about 75 books a week; science fiction, classics and issues of *National Geographic* magazine are in high demand, as are other non-fiction and reference works. With books donated from both private and corporate sources, a daily newspaper passing on unused review copies, the Footpath Book Club acts as a locus of community formation. The books it distributes provide its 'members' with a means to fill the boredom of the many unstructured hours that are the lot of the homeless, and 'a few books on an old shelf' can personalise the highly impersonal spaces of hostels and emergency accommodation (ibid.). Given these almost magical powers, it seems unlikely that books and reading should ever disappear. However, like other book readers, the Footpath Book Club's members are reading at a time when the future of books and reading is called repeatedly into question; a cultural form and practice that could be made first irrelevant, and then redundant, by digital culture. As Robert McCrum, now retired literary editor of *The Observer*, wrote recently: the universe of the book 'has been turned inside out by the biggest revolution since William Caxton set up his printing shop in the precincts of Westminster Abbey' (2008: electronic source). In such a time, a book about the contemporary culture of reading might soon find itself placed on a shelf marked 'cultural history'. It is a strange time to be writing a book about reading; we are reading in interesting times.

Optimists like book historian Steven Roger Fischer suggest that, alongside new technologies, fiction and non-fiction reading 'will continue to advance along with civilization' and therefore 'doubtless the same reading genres will live on: the novel, biography, travel guide, history and so on' (2003:342). Similarly, and with a sobriety that's not often a feature of this debate, David Carter writes that while new cultural forms do not replace existing ones, they do 'shuffle their place and purpose in the cultural field' (2008: electronic source), and so books will continue to exist but only while 'they still have utility, readability, marketability and authority' (ibid.). That old, middle-aged and new cultural technologies can productively coexist is demonstrated clearly by the BBC's World Book Club which, through a synergy of print, radio and internet, 'has been uniting millions of readers from all corners of the globe every month for more than five years' (bbc.co.uk).

Less sanguine about the coexistence of digital and print technology and far more bullish about the particular value of reading is the pugnacious William Gass who asserts that:

> if readers abandon reading to swivel-hip their way through the interbunk, picking up scraps of juicy data here and there and rambling on the email in that new fashion of grammatical decay, the result will be to make real readers, then chief among the last who are left with an ability to reason, rulers. Books made the rich richer. Books will make the smart smarter (Gass 1999: electronic source).

Others are, however, far less certain about the book's longevity. Forty years after publishing *The Uses of Literacy*, Richard Hoggart observes with obvious sadness that books:

> are beginning to seem archaic, left on the roadside. Strange that we have been brought to asking: who will go on reading? Who will retain the memories? Even stranger that people such as I, hoisted by books into a deeper and richer world than I could in childhood have ever imagined, may now be looking at a depopulating landscape (1999:197).

For every critic or scholar who looks to the possibilities that books will exist productively along with the internet there are others, like Sven Birkerts in *The Gutenberg Elegies: The Fate of Reading in an Electronic Age* (1994), who consider the book and reading's imminent passing as a marker of declining overall literacy, an indicator of the coarsening of cultural life, or even a portent of impending cultural crisis: 'as the world hurtles on toward its mysterious rendezvous' with its digital future, 'the old act of reading a serious book becomes an elegiac exercise' (1994:6). Birkerts and his follow-travellers will not be cheered by the knowledge that five of Japan's best-selling novels of 2007, the first three included, were initially created to be read on mobile phones, before later publication in the more traditional form (Carter 2008: electronic form).

A recent US study published by the National Endowment for the Arts (NEA), makes many such gloomy prognostications about the future of book-reading. The ominously titled *Reading at Risk* (2004) offers solid statistical proof that 'literary reading', by which the compilers mean not the reading of literature, but reading for pleasure in general, is in terminal decline: '*Reading at Risk* is testimony that a cultural legacy is disappearing, especially among younger people' (NEA 2004:xii). Compared to oral culture or the electronic media, the report argues, 'print culture offers irreplaceable forms of focused attention and contemplation that make complex communications and in-sights possible. To lose such intellectual capability—and the many sorts of human continuity it allows—would constitute a vast cultural impoverishment' (ibid.). More widely, the report argues, 'the long term implications of this study not only affect literature but all the arts, as well as social activism such as volunteerism, philanthropy and even political engagement (ibid.). But in parallel with such discourses of decline, the booksellers' shelves appear, somewhat paradoxically, to be overloaded with general interest books about fiction and reading. It is possible that reading about reading novels might be more popular than novel-reading itself?

Not only are there many of these 'meta-books', but there are also many different types. Some, like Nicholas A. Basbanes' *Every Book its Reader: the Power of the Printed Word to Stir the World* (2005), in which the author argues elegantly for the continued relevance and value of book-reading in the information age, seem simultaneously reassuring and anachronistic. A second kind of meta-book advises the potential reader of the best books to read, like Peter Boxall's *1001 Books You Must Read Before You Die,* while a third group, of which literary critic Harold Bloom's *How to Read and Why* (2001) is a good example, goes one stage further and tells the reader not just what to read, but how to read. After providing his readers with five reading principles, ranging from 'clear your mind of academic cant', echoing Samuel Johnson, through 'one must be an inventor to read well', and on to the 'recovery of the ironic', Bloom accompanies the novice reader through the 'difficult pleasure' of reading the literary canon (2001:29). We must read such novels, Bloom suggests, 'as they were read in the eighteenth and nine-teenth centuries: for aesthetic pleasure and for spiritual insight' (2001:144). The decline in the position of books and reading within society in general has seemingly robbed the contemporary public of the cultural sensibility required to select and read a novel unaided.

At first it is difficult to comprehend why these 'remedial' books, as they have been patronisingly described by one novelist (Falconer 2007:7), are so popular at a time when interest in reading is apparently subsiding. On the one hand, these meta-books appear to be examples of 'functional books', where the reader 'follows step-be-step instructions, tempted by a tantalising glimpse of the piece's apparent climax and denouement' (Young 2007:50). On the other, the legions of reading guides assume the mantle of 'anti-books … the boy bands of the publishing world, cynical creations, manufactured for marketing reasons only' (Young 2007:50). Yet, one may argue that this proliferation of books about reading is not a paradox at all but in fact a logical outcome of the contemporary *mise en scène*, logical because 'our target-driven, sound-bite era favours a cut to the chase: it seems we like to be told not only what the best books are but to go … straight to the highlights' (ibid.). In a desire to presumably save readers precious reading time, there are guides to establishing reading groups, a phenomenon that also seems strangely anachronistic in the world of Facebook, bestsellers about book clubs (like *Reading Lolita in Tehran* by Azar Nafisi (2003)), books by or about celebrity readers (Melvyn Bragg's *12 Books That Changed the World* (2005)), and there are even books that offer to teach readers how to pretend that they have read a book when they have not (Pierre Bayard's *How to Talk About Books You Haven't Read* (2007)), an indication that being able to display a knowledge of books might still possess some cultural cachet; books remain 'a reassuring backdrop against which we lead our electronic existence' (Spender 1995:62).

The NEA's bleak prognosis is reminiscent of another grim forecast made at another time in another country. In *The Long Revolution*, British cultural critic Raymond Williams's quotes from a letter written in 1518, a letter in which an English printer named Copeland explained to a gentleman-author that, while he would gladly print his manuscript, the author should however expect little public interest because, in the printer's professional opinion, 'bokes be not set by: there time is past, I gesse; The dyse and cardes, in drynkynge wyne and ale, Tables, cayles, and balles, they be sette a sale. Men lete thyr children use all such harlotry, That byenge of bokes they utterly deny' (cited in Williams 1965:178). In other words, the gentleman author should not expect significant sales as books are no longer valued because people are drawn to the dissolute pleasures of drinking and gambling, and that parents do not instil an interest in reading in their offspring. So, less than half a century after the first book was printed in England (1477), an English printer-publisher was already predicting that they had had their day. If Copeland's comments seem rather familiar to an early twenty-first century reader, then his reasons for the parlous state of reading are equally resonant: people are more interested in popular entertainment than books. As in *Reading at Risk*, book-reading in early sixteenth-century England was under siege from the distractions of popular culture (dice and cards are proxies for the internet and video games) and what's more the book's future will soon be guillotined by the impending arrival of a non-reading generation. In fact, in the preceding century, self-serving cultural mandarins had already forecast that the arrival of printing would mark the beginning of the end for books, as the ensuing multitude of cheap but poor quality publications would inevitably produce a 'million half-baked brains' (Gass 1999: electronic source). Williams regards Copeland's fatalism as the genesis of a now venerable tradition: 'there has hardly been a generation since', he writes, 'that has not lamented the imminent passing of the book' (1965:178-79). A particularly bizarre manifestation of this tendency finds Victorian commentators arguing that the invention of the pneumatic tyre would precipitate 'the end of the fireside reading circle by putting the whole family on bicycles' (Altick 1963:375). Between the arrival of the pneumatic tyre and the emergence of the internet it was television that threatened to reduce books and print culture to a 'residual epistemology' (Postman 1985:28). If books were ever to disappear, as they well might do, then two cultural traditions would be lost: book-reading and worrying about the future of book-reading.

Although this book is about contemporary readers and their books, it is not an intervention in Williams's perennial debate. While it may indeed indicate that the situation is not as dire as some may suggest, that is not its purpose. Neither is this book an attempt to defend books and reading against attacks. What this book does do, however, is to examine the nature of contemporary book-reading as it is experienced and understood by those for whom reading is part of their daily cultural routine, readers who would no doubt disagree that 'the book has become a peripheral, a literary fashion accessory for the few who join book clubs or go to writers' festivals' (Young 2007:5); readers who seem less concerned about the future of the book than the cultural commentariat.

It was once quite acceptable to make analytical comments about reading without any substantial consideration of the role of readers themselves; a move akin to studying dance without the dancers (Fish 1980:22). But, in focusing on the everyday practices of reading, this book is situated firmly within a tradition of scholarly work in the humanities that has come, since the 1960s, to see the reader 'not as the passive recipient but as the active producer of meaning' (Regan 1998:138). Research into popular culture has subsequently moved away from the text as the sole arbiter of meaning and value, and has rejected the critical tradition that regarded the audiences for mass-mediated popular culture as passive, unthinking 'cultural dupes', a passivity that was fundamental to the discursive operation of the high/low cultural binary. As a consequence of this turn toward the reader, formulations of the active media audience have become something of a cliché, simultaneously magical and banal (Morris 1988). If the perception of popular readers as cultural dupes proscribed their agency, the active audience model is

frequently charged with overstating readers' cultural autonomy, an overstate-
ment that leads to an uncritical cultural populism. The apparent myopia of
the populist perspective is underscored by political scientist Boris Frankel
(1992) who wryly suggests that: 'the problem with populists is that ... if they
had been in ancient Rome they would have celebrated the slaughter of
animals and Christians in the colosseum as "audience participation"' (Frankel
1992:84). Summoned to ward off the lingering spectres of F.R. Leavis and
Theodor Adorno, the Jekyll and Hyde of twentieth-century mass culture theory
for whom mass-mediated popular culture could lead only to a passive 'pseudo-
individuation' (Adorno) or cultural 'de-creation' (Leavis), the 'active audience'
trope is often applied so superficially that it provides few specific or meaningful details about the ways cultural products, and books in particular, are
actually used by the people who invest money and time in them: 'we know
that people read and we know that they read novels', writes Andrew Milner,
but 'what seems much less clear, however, is exactly what it is that they
make of the books they read' (2005:184).

Whatever it is that readers do with books, it is certainly much easier to
assert that they play an active role in the production of cultural meanings and
pleasures than it is to discover exactly what types of meanings and pleasures
are produced. As Tony Bennett and Janet Woollacott argue:

> most approaches to the problem of reading have amounted to little more
> than a series of no doubt well intended but nonetheless, largely gestural nods
> in the direction of the reader—a question of doing the same old thing, analyz-
> ing texts, and then say generously that, of course, interpretations may vary,
> even to the point of entertaining the prospect of unlimited semiosis (Bennett
> and Woollacott 1987:63).

Despite being made two decades ago, this point still holds true, so much so
that in his exhaustive cultural history of the reading of the British working-
class autodidact, Jonathan Rose still feels it necessary to point out the methodological limitations of those cultural studies' scholars who continue to try
'to discern the attitudes of the presumed audience by studying the texts they
are supposed to have read' (Rose 2001:367). Despite its complexity and
sophistication, and the over-determined nature of its subject, theorising the
role of the reader is a much more manageable and common scholarly project
than studying reading and readers empirically. Hence, in cultural studies'
discussions and analyses of popular print culture, the reading of real historical
subjects remains a minority interest.

In this book I try to avoid 'the same old thing' by examining what
'ordinary' readers actually do with their books; I look at the reading of fiction
as it occurs, almost unnoticed, in living and bedrooms, in parks, on the beach,
and on public transport; a popular reading culture distinct from that of

scholars and print professionals. To do more than surmise the *cultural* from the *textual*, this book uses an ethnographic method that allows researchers to examine what Paul Wills has called 'sunk signifiers'; to get closer to where the everyday meanings of reading are actually negotiated, the sensuous practices that make a life (2001:32).

Ethnographic methods have been used within cultural studies' research for some time. But while it is possible to locate the origins of the qualitative studies of books and reading in Q.D. Leavis's *Fiction and the Reading Public* (1932) and Richard Hoggart's *The Uses of Literacy* (1957), sustained ethnographic research has only been a staple of cultural studies' practice since the 1980s. At its heart, ethnographic work focuses on the relations within and between three elements: 'creative meaning-making in sensuous practice; forms, i.e. what the symbolic resources used for meaning are and how they are used; the social; the formed and forming relation to the main structural relations, necessities and conflicts of society' (Willis 2001:109). So, like text-based critics, cultural studies' ethnographers are still concerned with forms, 'the symbolic resources used', but they also look to embodied 'practice' and 'the social', when crafting their accounts of culture.

This shift away from deducing reading practices from the textual analysis of 'popular' texts toward an ethnography of embodied cultural practices produces a different perception of popular, or as I will refer to it, everyday reading. First, it is no longer productive to equate everyday reading to the consumption of putatively popular texts. Such a correlation would only perpetuate a crude high/low cultural binary, which is itself reliant upon an unproblematic hierarchy of texts, a text-determined conception of popular reading that also conveniently ignores both the everyday consumption of aesthetically-coded texts, like the novels of Jane Austen, and the intense academic readings of popular genres such as detective and science fiction. Everyday reading cannot be adequately conceived as the consumption of particular types of 'low-brow' books, and neither should we uncritically accept any definition that brackets everyday reading with a single reading position. Such a formulation, whether readers are theorised as 'resistant' or 'compliant', or whether they read for 'pleasure' or 'distraction' restricts the significance of 'popular' reading to meaning produced through the interpretation of narrative. To accept this view of 'popular' reading would overlook the possibility that books may have an everyday cultural or social significance that is not confined to the meaning of the narrative, and that individual cultural actors may be able to draw upon multiple reading protocols taken from different cultural domains. Finally, everyday reading is not the practice of a particular type or class of person; it is not the reading of the uneducated.

Neither the reading of 'popular' texts, nor a single reading position, or a class of reader, everyday reading is rather a reading practice that is negotiated within three interdependent socio-cultural economies: economies of time and space; of the social; and of the text. This book shows how the performances, meanings, values and uses of books, in short the experience of everyday reading, is shaped by these interlaced cultural economies.

The first of these economies, the spatio-temporal, shapes everyday reading practices because readers must continually create a place in which to read, a place that is never given but must be negotiated with, or taken from, others. And as everyday readers are forced to exploit liminal spaces, like public transport, spaces that might not even be considered cultural at all, everyday reading has a cultural geography distinct from that of the reading professional. While reading is most often a solo performance, this does not equate to reading being a socially isolated activity. Indeed, social networks play a highly significant in fashioning everyday readers' book culture because everyday reading also occurs within a social economy. The sociality that is accrued through book exchanges and conversation constitute informal communities of readers, and books provide fixed points about which a reader's identity may be negotiated—books operate to increases to readers' sociality, to extend an individual's 'funds of sociability' (Allen 1979) and act as an index of intimacy, a means to measure the depth and strength of a friendship. Finally, just as readers have to read within both spatio-temporal and social cultural economies, so they must also read within an economy of the text. The text becomes another context that determines the nature of everyday reading. Readers have preferences for particular authors and genres and read these novels through a number of discursive repertoires (Fish 1980; Hermes 1995). Using Toni Morrison's *Beloved* as a case study, a novel more often associated with high rather than popular culture, this book demonstrates how readers make narrative meaningful though the application of different interpretative frames. When theorised within these three zones of socio-cultural economy, the answers to any questions about what people do with their books take on an increasingly rich and sophisticated aspect.

Popular culture has become a commonplace term in the media, and it is used with little or no critical reflection. Scholars, however, do not get off so lightly: we must define our terms. So before providing a detailed investigation of these three cultural economies of everyday reading I want to take one step backward and begin where all studies of popular culture need start: the problem of definition. This book begins by grappling with three important questions. First, how to productively define popular culture; second, following on from the difficulties of defining popular culture, what is popular reading? And third, once we know what popular reading is, what is the most effective means to study it?

1 'Life after Text': The Analysis of Everyday Cultural Practices

Culture is one of the two or three most complicated words in the English language.

Raymond Williams, Keywords

The other very important thing to remember is that methodologies are merely tools. They are good servants but very poor masters.

Malcolm Crick and Bill Geddes, Research Methods in the Field: Eleven Anthropological Accounts

Introduction

Any study purporting to examine popular reading practices immediately runs into a problem: the problem of 'the popular'. Raymond Willliams places 'popular' alongside 'class', 'ideology' and 'hegemony', all words that are problematic because their 'meanings seemed to me inextricably bound up with the problems [they were] being used to discuss' (Williams 1976:13). The Latin root of 'popular' is *popularis* ('belonging to the people') and for much of its life the word appears to have had a derogatory usage, used to describe things that were 'low' or 'base'. Later, in the nineteenth century, 'popular' accrued a less negative connotation and was used in reference to phenomena that people considered 'widespread' or even 'well-liked' (Williams 1976:198-99). These two meanings, 'base' and 'widespread', have survived into the twenty-first century. It is this latter meaning of the popular that is invoked when commentators describe the Harry Potter books or *The Da Vinci Code* as 'popular reading'.

When used in combination with another of Williams' keywords, 'culture', the possible meanings of 'the popular' proliferate wildly. As Stuart Hall writes 'I have almost as many problems with "popular" as I have with "culture". When you put the two together the difficulties can be pretty horrendous' (Hall 1994:455). From one perspective, popular culture is an oxymoron because 'Culture', in the capitalised form, has been used to describe everything that is not 'of the people' nor 'widespread'; that is, everything that is *not* popular. To note this contradiction is just the beginning of further confusion over the meaning of popular culture because, as John Storey argues, 'any definition of popular culture will bring into play a combination of the different meanings of the term culture with different meanings of the term popular' (Storey 1997:7). Popular culture implies a considerable number of definitions, the uses of which depend upon the type of intellectual work waiting to be performed; popular culture is 'an empty conceptual category, one that can be filled in a wide variety of often conflicting ways depending on the context of use' (Storey 1997:1). In support of his argument, Storey provides six possible uses of 'popular culture': quantitative, residual, mass, romantic, resistant and postmodern. To this collection may be added the popular as 'consumption' (Douglas and Isherwood 1996), as an aesthetics of distraction (Chambers 1986), as mass mediated and symbolically derived entertainment (Fowles 1996), as 'fun' (Frith 1991) and as the 'everyday' (Lefebvre 1991; de Certeau 1984). So depending on one's definition, popular reading might be the reading of 'low brow' books, reading distractedly or reading for entertainment. With such a large range of possible definitions of the popular it is not surprising that some critics think that the best thing to do is reject the term altogether: Douglas Kellner, for example, speaks not of popular but of media culture (Kellner 1995).

This struggle to define 'the popular' is far more the concern of academics than cultural consumers. After all 'popular culture was not identified by *the people* but by others' (Williams 1976:199). This 'problem of the popular' is then a conundrum of method and purpose for institutionalised researchers and in an attempt to make sense of this proliferation of discourses Simon During offers three versions of the academic popular: centre-confirming, para-scientific and resistance (During 1990:489). It is through such approaches as these that popular culture has become a legitimate topic of academic research but in their efforts to legitimise the study of popular culture within the academy, practitioners have paid less attention than they probably should have to those who actually consume the 'popular' culture under investigation. Whether it is the psychoanalytic readings of children's television (Penley 1989), close reading of popular music lyrics (Cranney-Francis 1995; Cullen 1998), the 'literification' of popular film (Milner 2005), celebrations of 'semiotic guerrilla warfare' (Fiske 1989), or the comparison of Icelandic sagas and rap lyrics (Patrick 2008), the same question needs to be asked: whose meanings and values, whose culture, is being articulated through such analysis? The 'popular' culture that is produced through a text-centred approach indicates more perhaps about the struggle for the meaning of popular culture in the academy, than it does about popular cultural practices within the broader community.

What is everyday reading?

The limitation of such text-focused interpretations of the meaning of popular culture is indicated by Michele de Certeau who suggests that reading the cultural *off* the textual camouflages 'the exclusivity that it assures to reading practices confined to a given milieu. What it *states* conceals what it *does*, namely, prohibit all other interpretative practices' (de Certeau 1997:144). In professing the meaning of particular 'popular' novels, academic readers elide other non-academic interpretations, uses and affects of that novel, interpretations, uses and affects that such research is supposed to reveal. A strong case against the hegemony of the textualist tradition is made by media academics Joli Jensen and John Pauly:

> In the textualized versions of cultural studies, theorists stand in the place of evidence. Since Marx, or Freud, or Althusser, or Gramsci, or Foucault, or Derrida have offered us convincing accounts of a social order that the critic already knows to be true, merely quoting theorists can constitute proof of the validity of our interpretations. By this invocation of names, critics deliver a one-two punch, voicing arrogant, unquestioned faith in their theories, and an unrelenting disrespect for people's understandings that are not trustworthy, interesting or illuminating. The arrogance lies in the belief that, unlike other people, certain theorists have located and articulated what is real and what matters, not just about their own lives, but about everyone else's (Jensen and Pauly 1997:160).

Others like Stuart Hall (1999) and David Morley (1997) have also criticised the textualist orthodoxy. Morley opposes the 'tendency towards the textualization of cultural studies,' because it allows 'the cultural phenomenon under analysis to drift entirely free from their social and material foundations' (Morley 1997:123). More broadly, as Richard Johnson noted, 'all cultural products are "read" by persons other than professional analysts (if they weren't there would be little profit in their production), but we cannot predict these uses from our own analysis, or indeed, from the conditions of production' (Johnson 1987:46). The logical outcome of Johnson's position is that textual hermeneutics, regardless of its theoretical affiliations, is never a wholly adequate research method. Despite these limitations, however, the 'textual attitude' (Said 1980:112) remains a feature of academic studies of popular culture.

No doubt scholars of non-living cultures have little choice other than to turn to texts in their effort to reconstruct cultural meanings and affects. Those who investigate contemporary cultural consumption have, however, a wider choice of methodologies. The centrality of 'the text' in much cultural studies research could be a marker of the discipline's literary origin, but textual analysis as a research method appears increasingly limited if culture is defined more as a set of interrelated practices than the aesthetic and formal qualities of certain objects (Hall 1997:20). The need to see cultural texts as integral to and constitutive of cultural processes is stressed by Raymond Williams who argues that even though cultural texts 'are, in one sense, explicit and finished forms ... [they are] not only that because to complete their inherent process, we have to make them present, in specifically active "readings"' (Williams 1977:129). Reading and form in this critical appraisal are fused: the text requires a reading to be fully 'present', to be materially actualised within a particular historical moment, while readings (readers) need texts to enable a performance. This symbiosis of form and reading is articulated by Howard Becker who suggests that, unlike literary scholars, sociologists:

> realized early that it was a confusing error to focus on objects, as though the subjects of our investigation were tables or charts or ethnographies or movies. It makes more sense to see these [cultural] artefacts as the frozen remains of collective action, brought to life whenever someone uses them, as people making and reading charts or prose, making and seeing films. To speak of a film is shorthand for 'making or seeing a film' (Becker 1986:1).

Consequently, analysing books as derascinated texts will not reveal what the readership does with them; the meanings readers make and the pleasures they derive from reading cannot be articulated through textual analysis, and yet is in these 'specifically active readings' (Williams 1977:129) or 'creative re-articulations' (Johnson 2000:35) of books that popular or everyday reading is to be found.

The everyday reading of this book's title, a useful and more specific term that substitutes for the alternative popular reading, describes not the reading of 'lowbrow' books. The reassuring high/low binary that is often erected when the social and cultural are conflated should then be put aside in favour of a model that moves past neatly and conveniently correlated hierarchies of texts. Everyday reading, moreover, does not connote a single aesthetics of engagement with books, whether it is for pleasure or distraction, to resist or to conform. Furthermore, everyday reading is not the activity of a particular class of reading subject—popular reading does not describe the actions of the un- or the under-educated because, within contemporary consumer society, cultural commodities like novels are not the exclusive preserve of particular social groups or classes. Although there is some argument to suggest that this may have historically been the case (Burke 1978), books in particular have never been the exclusive domain of particular socio-cultural groups (Altick 1963; Rose 2001); even if they have been produced with a particular socio-cultural group in mind books have always been read by unintended audiences. Rather, everyday reading is a common practice that is embedded within and constitutive of readers' broader cultural and social lives. Readers' 'creative re-articulations' are always articulated to regimes that regulate meaning and value: aesthetic, educational and commercial. Importantly, everyday reading practices are circumscribed and shaped by spatio-temporal, social and textual economies that differ, sometimes radically, from those experienced by professional readers, even when they share similar books. These co-existing orders of reading, everyday and professional, use books that are shared within a society at large, but they are understood, valued and used in different ways (Chartier 1995:89). If textual hermeneutics cannot take researchers into the cultural economy of everyday reading then it needs to be replaced by a more felicitous research methodology: ethnography.

Why use an ethnographic method?

Ethnographic method, with its democratic imperative, has become increasingly part of cultural studies' methodological arsenal. In their search for a better way to understand the 'real readers' of popular women's fiction, Batsleer *et al* (1985) draw attention to the seductive pluralism of ethnographic methodology.[1] 'At first sight,' they suggest:

> an 'ethnography of readers' seemed to have enormous potential. Ethnography has an intensely democratic impulse, which provides a useful check against the temptation ... to speak too readily on others' behalf, and an acknowledgment of the obvious but easily neglected truth that any account of an activity that ignores or marginalises the experience and understanding of those directly engaged in it can hardly claim much accuracy or authenticity (Batsleer *et al*, 1985:146).

In contrast to the sophistication of textual analysis, enabled by increasingly arcane theories of culture and text, Christine Geraghty suggests that 'the tempting promise of ethnographic work is in the pragmatic appeal of its apparent premise. If you want to find out about audiences, why not ask them?' (Geraghty 1998:143). This appropriation has, however, also provoked much criticism (Radway 1988; Nightingale 1993; Murdock 1997). Cultural studies ethnographies have been variously criticised for their limited and limiting conception of the audience; their epistemological naiveté, and the attenuated cultural accounts some have produced; some ethnographic cultural studies, it is argued, pay only lip-service to the rigours of fieldwork. Moreover, the upsurge in cultural studies interest in ethnography in 1980s coincided with a profound reassessment of the method within one of its academic homelands: anthropology (Clifford and Marcus 1986). Of this reassessment John Van Maanen wrote that while it did 'not provide a better way to do ethnography,' it did 'remind us of the limits of representational possibilities and makes strong arguments to counter any faith in a simple or transparent world that can be known with any certainty' (Van Maanen 1995:18). Such criticisms and reappraisals notwithstanding, and without subscribing to a naïve realism, I would suggest that ethnographic method—the embodied interaction of researchers and cultural agents—can sensitise research into everyday cultural practices, like reading, in a manner that textual analysis alone cannot; it reconnects the cultural with the social and the material, and brings academic 'concepts into a relationship with the messiness of ordinary life' (Willis 2001:xi).

Four reasons to use an ethnographic method

Ethnographic method sensitises cultural research in four ways. First, ethnography allows researchers to investigate texts, objects and practices in the context of the cultural lives of the people that use them. As Ellen Seiter notes: 'The primary contribution of ethnographic audience research since the 1970s has been its demonstration that media consumption is embedded in the routines, rituals, and institutions—both public and domestic—of everyday life' (Seiter 1999:2; Morley and Silverstone 1992). Ethnographic accounts of cultural practices differ from those based on textual analysis because they often, but not always, exchange overt theoretical sophistication for richly rendered accounts of complex cultural lives. The appeal of ethnography is connected to its ability to represent the untidiness and ambiguities of culture: 'it seems better equipped to prise open for analysis the ambivalences of modernity in its present phase of development' (Drotner 1994:343).

Second, ethnography can provide the researcher with counter-knowledge. Because the method is founded on manufactured and contingent 'breakdowns', the points at which theory and experience diverge (Agar 1986:20), ethnography as a 'mechanism of consultation' (Johnson 2000:36) provides a basis upon which academic orthodoxies may be put on trial (Johnson 1998:5) and, if need be, amended, modified or corrected. Engagements with real people, the baseline of all qualitative or ethnographic research, 'challenge[s] the armchair sophistry of reader-response, reception aesthetics and spectatorship studies where researchers position themselves as the only viewers [or readers] that count' (Nightingale 1996:64). Ethnographic research may then counter academic assumptions about cultural practices because 'ethnographic work is always more complicated and diversified than our theories can represent ... The critical promise of the ethnographic attitude resides in its potential to make and keep our [academic] interpretations sensitive to concrete specificities, to history' (Ang 1996:110).

Despite the accent on specificity, ethnographers do make generalisations and the opinions of social and cultural agents are seen in the light of other material (Jankowski and Wester 1992:62; Geraghty 1998:155). In this book, material produced during interviews is used in combination with other orders of discourse: large scale quantitative research data, material taken from other ethnographies, and research from a wide range of academic disciplines including literary and cultural studies, cultural and social history, cultural geography, sociology and anthropology. These forays into other disciplines are necessary because the discussions with readers raised issues that were not in any way respectful of the neat, if often arbitrary, academic boundaries within which research is executed: the interviewees pushed the research into unfamiliar territory. Finally, when generalisations are made from such local ethnographic studies, when micro- and macro-worlds are connected, I would suggest that such generalisations are less totalitarian, or at least more permeable to different interpretations, because they are products of self-consciously specific surroundings. As Morley and Silverstone note, 'ethnographic accounts are essentially contestable, just as cultural analysis is a necessarily incomplete business of guessing at meanings, assessing the better guesses, and drawing explanatory conclusions from the better guesses' (Morley and Silverstone 1992:157).

The opportunity for 'surprise' is the third sensitising feature of ethnographic methodology. As Paul Willis argued over thirty years ago, ethnographic method has the capability to surprise researchers, allowing them to reach knowledge not prefigured in their starting paradigm (Willis 1990a:90). Ann Gray (1997) adds a post-structuralist twist to Willis's formulation by recasting 'surprise' as 'self-reflexivity'; this self-reflexivity is manifest through the process of actually conducting research. Consequently, ethnographic work has the tendency to mutate, to become something other that it was supposed to be as the researcher's control over the research process is to some extent lessened. Despite the numerous methodological and meta-ethnographical publications now circulating, it is wrong to legislate away the pragmatic nature of direct encounters with people and communities through the adoption of iron-clad methods (Crick and Geddes 1998:2) because the actual process of interaction may override, or re-order, even the most rigorously theorised research project. This pragmatism is a positive phenomenon because it is in these instances that research starts to bear the imprint of the cultures under investigation, as methods evolve to suit the particular research situation.[2] The veracity of an ethnographic study is, after all, not found in its methodology but in the cultural account that is produced. Though important, method is only one factor that contributes to the overall project (Wellman 1994:569).

Finally, ethnography is a sensitising research method because it forces researchers to meet their others, and as researchers come face-to-face with their others, so they also come face-to-face with the ethics of cultural research. An epistemological and ethical duality is a feature of all cultural criticism, however in most research methods greater emphasis is usually placed on the former. While acknowledging the inescapable problem of representation, Diane Elam sees the ethical dimension of research as possibly more significant than the epistemological:

> Trying to do justice to the other, trying not to appropriate the other's discourse, is an unresolvable epistemological bind—which still does not mean that we stop trying to be just. Rather, the significance of this predicament lies in an *ethical* not an epistemological recognition: the recognition that there is no guilt-free speech (Elam 1995:235).

Researchers will always represent others, be tied by 'the unresolvable epistemological bind' because: 'there is no neutral place to stand free and clear in which one's words do not prescriptively affect or mediate the experience of others, nor is there a way to decisively demarcate a boundary between one's location and all others' (Alcoff 1991:20). There is, in short, 'no principled resolution, no alternative, to the problems of speaking for others' (Roth cited in Richardson 1995:215). Researchers are then bound to 'do justice' to those for whom they are speaking, over and above the quandary of representation. According to Stephen Muecke, researchers need 'to assert [their] limited regimes of truth and see how they match up to challenges' (Muecke 1993:329). Without direct access to others' experiences, actions, or existence, all the researcher can do is to represent, translate and comprehend the other across the intersubjective border (Knauft 1994:122). Researchers need to allow for the self-reflexivity of their subjects, to acknowledge their informants' ability to think—politically, historically and theoretically—about their own lives (Lovatt and Purkiss 1995:2; Gray 1997:103). Yet, when gaps in experience are evident they need to be respected and understood (Shaffir 1999:683). Ethnographers are reminded constantly of the ethical dimension to cultural research through their direct dealings with real others. I would argue that a change in methodology has a profound effect on the way in which researchers write about cultural practices; it is one thing to dismiss or romanticise the culture of others from the comfort of a university office, but it is quite another to do the same after contact with people who live those cultures.

Ethnography and reading in cultural studies: from *Fiction and the Reading Public* (1932) to *Book Clubs* (2003)

In anthropology and sociology ethnography has a venerable tradition, whereas it has only relatively recently made safe its position within the canon of cultural studies' research methodologies. The origin of ethnography in British cultural studies is most commonly located in Richard Hoggart's *The Uses of Literacy* (1957). This text, along with Raymond Williams's *Culture and Society* (1958), marks the beginning of a significant change in the conception of culture, a movement away from thinking of culture as a moral phenomenon towards a more anthropological conception. However, before I examine ethnographic cultural studies in terms of popular reading, some attention must be paid to an overlooked, and perhaps surprising, antecedent to Richard Hoggart's work: Q.D. Leavis's *Fiction and the Reading Public* (1932).

The sociology of the herd

Q.D. Leavis and her survey of the production and readership of popular fiction are often cited, not as intellectual forebears, but as the apotheosis of everything that is wrong with the 'culture and civilization tradition'. Invoked mainly for the purpose of ridicule, the work of Q.D. Leavis and her husband F.R. Leavis now provide something of a negative example to newer generations of scholars; they represent everything that cultural studies is, or should be, against. Unsurprisingly, contemporary interpretations of *Fiction and the Reading Public* are largely hostile towards Q.D. Leavis's attempt to deal 'with fiction as distinct from literature' (Leavis 1932:xiv). However, if contemporary readers can accept and see past the now obvious shortcomings of her analysis, they will see that Q.D. Leavis's study prefigures later developments in the practice of empirically based and other branches of popular culture studies: 'it must be remembered,' argues Storey, 'that from a historical point of view, the [Leavisite] tradition's work is absolutely foundational to the project of the study of popular culture within British cultural studies' (Storey 1997:42). Bob Ashley agrees with Storey that: '*Fiction and the Reading Public* was [a] ... genuinely pioneering study of new territory. ... [r]esponses ought ... to go beyond the unhistorical "Queenie-bashing"' (Ashley 1997:33).

Read in a less confrontational and more historical light it is possible to see a number of issues in *Fiction and the Reading Public* that, although embryonic in development, would later manifest themselves in many sophisticated forms. Q.D. Leavis emphasises the need to examine contemporary culture: 'to be interested in cultural questions is necessarily to set out from the contemporary situation, and I have organised the results in accordance with this principle' (Leavis 1932:xv). She also advocates interdisciplinary study within the humanities (Leavis 1932:272). However, in the context of ethnographically-based cultural studies, the most important element of Queenie Leavis's analysis is her choice of an 'anthropological methodology' (Leavis 1932:xiv).

John Docker insists that Leavis adopts an anthropological method because in her opinion popular fiction is 'certainly not worthy of being called literature, and certainly not worthy of detailed literary analysis' (Docker 1994:24). Such an anthropological or sociological approach to popular fiction is, indeed, indicative of modernist criticism's othering of mass mediated popular culture. Lacking the critical distance of literature or art, mass mediated popular culture cannot provide what Adorno describes as 'negative knowledge': an epistemological position from which to critique actuality (Forgacs 1992:189). In much modernist discourse, mass mediated popular culture is represented, repeatedly, as part of an unambiguously negative process of modernisation: a corollary of urbanisation, consumerism, democracy, mass production, mass literacy and leisure.

From this perspective it is difficult to defend *Fiction and the Reading Public* against its detractors. Q.D. Leavis certainly locates popular fiction, and its readership, in a debased social world: patrons of lending libraries' 'stock of worn and greasy novels' are likened to drug addicts, modern language 'has no artistic possibilities' and the reading public 'has no means of knowing what it really thinks or feels ...', because their minds have been corrupted by 'films, magazines, newspaper and best-sellers' (Leavis 1932:244). Moreover, the ideology driving Leavis toward fieldwork is far removed from that of her transatlantic contemporaries in the Chicago school of urban ethnography. For while the followers of Robert Park saw fieldwork as an agent of social critique and change (Van Maanen 1988:18), Q.D. Leavis uses it for elitist and reactionary purposes: to provide a 'sociology of the herd'.

In her transition from literary critic to pseudo-anthropologist Leavis articulates, albeit unintentionally, the limitations of textual analysis as a method of cultural enquiry. 'Clearly,' argues Leavis, 'both [analytical] methods, the critic's and the scholar's need to be supplemented by a third, a novel pulled up as a unit for inspection clings with its tentacles round so many non-technical matters that it cannot always be safely severed from them' (Leavis 1932:xiv). And it is too these 'tentacles' of popular fiction that much of her book is devoted: publishers, authors as businessmen, journalism, book retailing and the operation of the lending libraries, all 'non-technical matters' that now, eighty years hence, fall well within conventional academic parameters. This methodological change from textual to anthropological analysis, although severely compromised by snobbery, enlarges the object of study considerably and provokes different cultural questions. For instance, by employing an anthropological method the critic may consider novels as elements in a wider social world: 'what part do they [popular novels] play in the lives of the readers of the *Sunday Dispatch?*' Leavis asks (1932:37). Consequently, the meaning of a text is now located in the social domain, it is constituted in a social act, as well as in the realms of narrative or linguistic interpretation. It seems that Q.D. Leavis here displays a better grasp of what is required then many of the so-called progressive or radical scholars who have succeeded her.

While it is certainly wrong to overlook or dismiss out of hand Q.D. Leavis's study, it is also a mistake to overstate its significance. The potential of her anthropological method is never realised. Leavis makes no direct contact with any readers of mass circulation fiction and so she remains imprisoned within a narrow ideological definition of culture and value: she is never open to her other. The quantitative and qualitative method adopted in *Fiction and the Reading Public* is simply a search for Williams's 'illustrative instances' (1981:34), a quest to prove the decadence of British culture and, as a corollary, the urgent need for a defensive and discriminating minority: *Fiction and the Reading Public* merely provides empirical grist for the Leavisite mill. Before an anthropological or ethnographic approach can reveal the social meanings of cultural practices, culture has to be defined in a different way, and before such a redefinition can be achieved there needs to be a similar reconsideration of the purpose of cultural analysis. Such a fundamental reconceptualisation of the meaning of culture was unthinkable for either Leavis and for many others like them.

In the early writings of Raymond Williams and Richard Hoggart however, such a redefinition does occur and, therefore, the horizon of cultural studies is widened. Abstract hegemonic discourses of authenticity and exclusion are challenged by an understanding based on proximity, plurality and exchange. Culture, for Hoggart and Williams, ceases to be 'a study of perfection' (Arnold 1973:166) and neither is it the property of an increasingly uncommon literary and moral language, as it was for F.R. Leavis; 'Culture' is now culture and as the famous dictum has it, 'culture is ordinary'. For Williams, culture, and by implication value, is to be found in almost every human endeavour (Williams 1965:61). The product of this transition from a claustrophobic literary to a broad anthropological definition of culture is a change in the mode of cultural analysis. Williams articulates this move in analytical approach when a social definition of culture is adopted. The analysis of culture, from such a definition, is the clarification of meanings and values implicit and explicit 'in a particular way of life, a particular culture' (Williams 1965:58). The argument that the adoption of an anthropological definition of culture results in an anthropological method of cultural analysis is evident in Richard Hoggart's *The Uses of Literacy* (1957). In this influential book, Hoggart brings together two concepts that would later become crucial to subsequent cultural studies, ethnographic or otherwise: the centrality of context to understandings of cultural consumption and the active nature of the audience for popular culture.

Retrospective participant observation: *The Uses of Literacy*

Aiming as he does to relate 'particular aspects' of working-class lives 'to the wider life they live' Hoggart appears to advocate a form of cultural analysis akin to Geertzian 'thick description'. Clifford Geertz argues that anthropologists ' have to try to see beyond habits to what the habits stand for, to see through the statements to what the statements really mean (which may be the opposite of the statements themselves),' and, just as Geertz desires to get behind 'the wink' and dig down through the 'hierarchy of meaningful structures' in which actions are 'produced, perceived and interpreted', (Geertz 1973:7), so Hoggart's goal is 'to detect the differing pressures of emotion *behind* idiomatic phrases and ritualistic observances' (Hoggart 1957:17 my emphasis). The context of consumption, therefore, becomes fundamental to the study of culture and it continues to be a crucial and problematic consideration in current ethnographically based cultural studies.

Similarly, the trope of the 'active audience' has become something of a talisman in cultural and media studies (Ang 1996; Nightingale 1996). In anticipation of such interest, Hoggart stresses the need to consider 'the attitudes they [the working-class] bring to their entertainment.' Unlike those in the culture and civilisation tradition, Hoggart argues passionately that the working-classes are *actively* involved in the production of their culture: 'the working-class have a strong natural ability to survive change by *adapting* or *assimilating* what *they* want in the new and *ignoring* the rest' (Hoggart 1957:32, my emphasis). Indeed, it is this ability that Hoggart suggests is under threat from newer forms of mass culture. By accentuating the transformative nature of working-class cultural practices Hoggart foreshadows the work of both de Certeau (1984), of 'making over', and the autonomous symbolic economy of Fiske (1989).

The first half of *The Uses of Literacy* could be considered retrospective participant observation. In its intoxicating combination of experiential authenticity and subjective partiality, Hoggart's representation of the cultural *mise en scene* is 'based to a large extent on personal experience, and does not purport to have the scientifically-tested character of a sociological survey' (Hoggart 1957:9). Hoggart freely acknowledges that his analysis of working-class life is subjective and open to challenge: 'I have also noted one or two instances in which others, with experience similar to mine, think differently,' (ibid.) and elsewhere, when considering the effects of his working-class identity, he confesses that:

> this very emotional involvement presents considerable dangers ... in writing I found myself constantly having to resist a strong inner pressure to make the old much more admirable than the new, ... Presumably some kind of nostalgia was colouring the material in advance: I have done what I could to remove its effects (Hoggart 1957:17).

This comment is an admission that the effects of the personal and the political could not be removed from his analysis. As a result, his speaking from experience and his (now fashionable) self-reflexivity operates quite paradoxically; it confers and destabilises his text's authority.

In his interpretation of the working-class culture of the 1930s Hoggart both critiques and defends the culture of his youth. This is demonstrated in his discussions of various working-class cultural practices (drinking, gambling, even prostitution) that, despite high levels of bourgeois indulgence, attracted condemnation from the moral majority. In his discussion of working-class reading of the period he is keen to defend some popular magazines against allegations that they are nothing but 'crude' and 'sensational' (1957:121). Rather than socially deracinating cultural artefacts as a prelude to judgement against a universal and objective measure of culture and morality, Hoggart interprets reading and other cultural practices within the context of everyday life.

Unfortunately, in the second half of *The Uses of Literacy*, Hoggart does return to just such an orthodox critique of mass culture. In his shift from sympathetic cultural anthropologist to dogmatic mass culture critic, Hoggart shows little regard for many aspects of contemporary (1950s) working-class life or the wider social world in which they operate. He speaks of the 'endless rain of confetti-literature' falling on the family (1957:240); describes 'gangster-fiction' as 'the popular literature of an empty megapolitan world' (1957:270); and worries about the 'proportions of the issues of public libraries [that] are of worthless fiction' (1957:332). The anthropological definition of culture, if not completely discarded, is eclipsed here by the moral as Hoggart returns to conservative formulations of meaning and value (Storey 1997:51). In this left-Leavisite mode, Hoggart is guilty of the sins that he warns others against: the inadequate consideration of the social, spatial and political contexts of everyday cultural practices. He widens the gap between researcher and researched; the fragmented, erotic 'looks' of culturalist ethnography are exchanged for the pornographic gaze of the aloof modernist critic.[3] These criticisms aside it was *The Uses of Literacy* 'more than any other publication [that] shifted the cultural debate in Britain from a stark opposition between elitist minority culture and lowly mass culture towards a serious engagement with the value and the values of majority cultural experience' (McGuigan 1992:49).

Although their motivations were very different, both Q.D. Leavis and Hoggart attempted to analyse the meaning and function of cultural texts, including books, within their social contexts. But during the 1970s and 1980s, the practitioners of ethnographic cultural studies seemed largely to lose interest in books as subcultures (Hall and Jefferson 1976; Grimshaw, Hobson and Willis 1980) and television audiences (Morley 1980; Ang 1982; Hobson

1982) came to dominate research. It is dangerous to speculate as to why books and reading became unfashionable. One reason might be that ethnographic researchers were trying to distance themselves from the literary roots of cultural studies and more traditional English literary scholarship generally. Another might be that book reading was seen as middle-class cultural activity and therefore too conservative a subject for cultural studies' left-leaning political commitments (Jensen and Pauly 1997:166).

Despite the dominant position of subcultural and television research during this period, the book was not totally neglected. While the new audience studies experiment was under way in Britain, in the United States Janice Radway published *Reading the Romance* (1984), an ethnographic study of the female readership of romance novels. In a recent reappraisal of this work, Helen Wood suggests that '*Reading the Romance* should be remembered for securing the possibility that some of the most fruitful insights into culture can be gained by stepping out of the disciplining structures that are often reinforced in the institutionalisation and bureaucratisation of the academy' (Wood 2004:147).

Janice Radway and the Smithton women

Reading the Romance was inspired by a set of theoretical questions that coalesced around the 'social and hence variable nature of semiotic processes' (Radway 1991:4). If reading varies historically, and we wish to use books to say something about society then 'it would be necessary to connect particular texts with the communities that produced them and to make some effort to specify how the individuals involved actually constructed those texts as meaningful semiotic structures' (ibid.). Having accepted this position, Radway came to the conclusion that American studies needed ethnographies of reading (ibid.). In this desire to link text and community, she began her research not with a defined social group, as might be expected from a more 'sociological' method, but with a particular genre of fiction. Concerned by the production and distribution arrangements that govern the availability of romance novels, like Q.D. Leavis before her, Radway wrestles with the 'tentacles' of popular fiction. Radway suggests that, when considering romance novels as mass-market products, literary critics in their obsession with texts pay far too little attention to the material and social forces that frame textual production (Radway 1991:19). From her analysis of the sites of material production, she moves on to consider readers' acts of creative consumption. Through the use of individual and group interviews, and written surveys, she is introduced to the culture of a group of women romances readers who 'feel guilty about spending money on books that are regularly ridiculed by the media, their husbands and their children' (Radway 1991:54). Finally, Radway returns to the firmer ground of textual analysis, with a critical comparison of failed and ideal romance novels.

Most significantly, Radway attends to these details with little, if any, of the uncritical consumerist reverie so often associated with the study of popular culture in the 1980s. Sensitive to 'the singularity of readers' (Radway 1991:53) she catalogues in considerable detail the evaluative criteria that her collaborators have developed to account for their likes and dislikes and to differentiate between and within genres. The readers articulate what romance reading means to them, within their own lives. Most significantly, Radway draws an important distinction between 'the meaning of the act [of reading] and the meaning of the text as read' (Radway 1991:210), a difference that exposes the contradiction at the heart of the Smithton Women's reading practice. While the socially constituted act of reading enables 'the women to refuse momentarily their self-abnegating social role [...] the romance's narrative structure embodies a simple recapitulation and recommendation of patriarchy and its constituent social practices and ideologies (ibid.). Romance reading is then a fundamentally ambivalent activity, the pleasurable experience it affords is both a palliative to the emotional and romantic 'deprivation' (Radway 1991:70) of women's everyday experience and an assertion of the 'possibility' of an ideal heterosexual relationship (Radway 1991:221).

As a result of this ambivalence Radway's notion of cultural resistance, as it manifests itself in the reading practices of the Smithton women, has far more in common with the approach of the Birmingham School than it does the cultural populists. The explication of the contradiction between social and narrative meaning and appreciation of the complexity of reading a supposedly mundane fictional form is facilitated by Radway's willingness to give up her 'obsession with textual features and narrative details', in order that she better 'understand [the readers'] view of romance reading' (Radway 1991:86). This move away from formalist modes of analysis casts the researcher into the cultural domain of real, not just textual, others.

Despite its favourable reception (Cawelti 1986) and its status as a classic study 'that proves the value of ethnography in analyzing popular culture' (Abu-Lughod 1999:112), *Reading the Romance's* critics outnumber its imitators (Jenkins 1992; Hermes 1995; Ang 1996; Curran 2002; Wood 2004). For Ang, the pluralistic aims of the study and its method are undermined by its 'recruitist' feminism and 'political moralism' (Ang 1996:104). Radway also fails to critique her relationship with her informants and does not adequately differentiate their views from her own, a matter which is not helped by the pronounced lack of direct quotations from her interviews: the readers are given little opportunity to speak of themselves, a major weakness in any ethnographic work. Furthermore, Henry Jenkins, who otherwise regards *Reading the Romance* as 'exemplary', upbraids the author for casting 'writers as

vanguard intellectuals who might lead the fans toward a more overtly political relationship to popular culture' (Jenkins 1992:6). The final purpose of
Radway's study seems to be judgemental and didactic, rather than dialogic
and democratic; she 'retain[s] [her] intellectual pretensions and institutional
privileges' throughout (ibid.). Leaving aside such contrary views some of the
most telling criticisms of *Reading the Romance*, especially those related to
theory and methodology, are provided by Radway herself. In her introduction to the second edition, she outlines a number of considerations that
would need to be addressed 'were I writing *Reading the Romance* today'
(Radway 1991:5-6), and elsewhere Radway has praised anthropology's more
self-conscious approach to its methods and its attempts 'to theorize, among
other things, the nature of the relationship between culture and social
behaviour, the epistemological status of 'data' gathered in the field, the nature of 'experience' itself, and the status of explanatory social theories im-
ported from the ethnographer's own cultural universe' (Radway 1988:363).
Despite these reconsiderations ethnographic method remains a fundamental
part of Radway's research arsenal because it insists 'that the social is *always*
actively constructed by living subjects' (Radway 1988:373).

Reading the detectives

Like Radway, Joke Hermes' 'Cultural Citizenship and Crime Fiction' (2000)
also examines the readership of a popular fiction genre: this time detective
fiction. And again like Radway, Hermes is concerned with the relationship
between reading, genre and feminism. 'We wished,' she writes, 'to know
whether feminism had become part of how readers discuss and evaluate
mystery novels' (Hermes 2000:216). Hermes outlines three aims for her
research: to determine whether detective novels provide a vehicle for the
discussion of social issues; to see if they offer a form of social subjectivity via
the membership of a particular interpretative community; and finally to as-
certain if the genre presents women readers with new forms of feminist
identification. While the readers indicated that detective novels did provide
them with anthropological, historical and sociological knowledge as well as
entertainment, in her other two aims Hermes' findings took her wide of the
mark. Certainly, membership of an interpretative community did provide a
form of social subjectivity but it was not feminist but 'middle-class' because
'crime readers want to be liberal, self-styled middle-class professionals'
(Hermes 2000:228) and, therefore, they deploy a regime of value that separates them and their chosen genre from the readers of more mainstream
books, however defined. Moreover, when looking for feminist identification,
the author seems surprised, even disappointed, at the level of readers' political and gender conservatism: 'the interviews ... show feminism as relatively

marginal to the pleasures of and reasons for reading' (Hermes 2000:217). So, while in Hermes' opinion 'textual analysis claims convincingly that specific subgenres in crime fiction can be deemed feminist … the readers we interviewed make clear that there is no direct link between academic interpretation and accounts of everyday use' (Hermes 2000:219). This disjunction is a clear instance of ethnography's capacity to generate 'counter-knowledge', as real readers contradict the accepted wisdom of feminist media scholars.

Using as she does Stanley Fish's concept of the interpretative community, Hermes considers the social dimension to reading (reading protocols, readers' identities, and the socially negotiated hierarchies of value), but she does not go as far as to investigate, in any detail, how books and reading operate as part of more general social and cultural networks. Hermes does signal that she is interested in books as more than 'pleasurable texts' (2000:217), but she still concentrates on readers' use of narrative, or with a book's *content* at the level of text: this is made clear in her three aims outlined above: all are fixated with readers' relationship to narrative or interaction enabled by narrative. As a result any substantial reference to the cultural geography of reading is missing; where and when readers read detective fiction, although mentioned very briefly, are not considered significant.

Baby-boomers and their books

While Radway (1984) and Hermes (2000) situate a particular fiction genre at the centre of inquiry, genre is not the only way to focus an ethnographic study of reading. A small Australian study takes a different approach, its emphasis not on a text or genre, but a particular demographic of reader. In *Reading Professional Identities* (1995), and working at least partly within the parameters of cultural policy studies, Patrick Buckridge, Pamela Murray and Jock Macleod undertake an investigation of the reading practices of a small group of professional Australians aged between forty and fifty. In contrast to *Reading the Romance*, constrained by its overt feminism, Buckridge, Murray and Macleod are not limited by an overarching theoretical position. Instead, their aims were much broader: to find out the nature of 'baby-boomer' recreational reading; in the relationship between leisure reading and the requirements of professional practice (Buckridge *et al* 1995:2). The authors want 'not to isolate a "pure" reading practice, untainted by the academy, but to increase the visibility of other conditioning factors in the formation of reading behaviour' (Buckridge *et al* 1995:4).

Well aware of the limitations of any generalisations made from a small study of 25 readers, the researchers are nonetheless prepared to draw some 'tentative and open-ended' conclusions (Buckridge *et al* 1995:37). The authors conclude that, even within such a homogeneous group, 'there appears to be a wide variety of ways in which readers value books, relate them to the rest of their lives, and read them' (ibid.). Regardless of the manner in which books are used, the study uncovered reading practices that are overwhelmingly solitary, in terms of both its actual performance and as a social phenomenon. Moreover, while readers seemed aware of the importance of the literary canon, they were generally not well informed as to its content; the idea rather than the content of the canon 'may have important effects within specific class or occupational cultures' (Buckridge *et al* 1995:38). Surprisingly perhaps, the study found that 'over-reading' of the kind associated with literary analysis may occur without formal literary training, hence scholars and policy makers need to take account of 'the diversity of acquisition routes' of such reading skills. Finally, readers seem to have little or no national 'dimension of reading' (Buckridge *et al* 1995:39).

Like *Reading the Romance*, it is possible to criticise *Reading Professional Identities* for not allocating enough space to the discourse of their subjects. The authors do provide some lengthy extracts from interview transcripts, most often though they are content with very brief extracts or paraphrases. Like Radway too, Buckridge, Murray and Macleod draw a line between reading as a social and reading as a textual practice but the significance of reading as a social act is generally underplayed and is featured mainly in the form of background information. These issues aside, however, the most significant criticism of *Reading Professional Identities* may be levelled against the authors' decision to present readers with three specific texts 'to be read', rather than base their study upon their subjects' accumulated book knowledge.

In order to provide a textual focus for their study, the authors gave their readers three texts, their reading of which would later form the substance of a second research interview. Through contingency rather than design 'none of the participants had previously read any of the three works.' (Buckridge *et al* 1995:8), a 'fortuitous' state of affairs because this lack of prior engagement with the chosen texts 'may have made for somewhat more meaningful response-comparisons' (ibid.). This methodological choice differs from most cultural studies' ethnographies, including my own, which have generally approached an interpretative community though its texts and practices, or a text or practice through its interpretative community. In this case, the researchers investigate an interpretative community through texts that have not been previously an element in its reading culture.

This position may be justified in the sense that it may allow for a more effective comparison between readers' general reading processes. However, such a method connects readers to particular books, not through acts of everyday reading, but through the medium of an academic research project. The readers approach these texts *knowing* that they have, at a later date, to discuss them with an academic researcher. The possible effects of this research strategy and its associated power imbalance are not really addressed in the study. Readers may be able to provide detailed responses to the questions posed, and this information may be used to draw useful conclusions about their reading but the degree of congruity between these responses and actual everyday reading culture is open to question. Although the authors do not address this particular aspect of their method, they are nonetheless aware of the other methodological objections that critics may make to their findings: the small number of readers, the 'uncontrolled groups', and the 'flexible interview schedules' are all expected to draw criticism. While accepting these methodological limitations, the authors argue that 'there are clear justifications for collecting information this way. ... the information is almost certainly unobtainable by other, more quantitative methods' (Buckridge et al 1995:2). Here, I would agree with the authors and add that such information would not be available to text-only methods either, although this fact is never really acknowledged as a methodological shortcoming.

Book clubs: the social nature of reading

Rather than the now common approach to studying readers, where one begins within either a particular genre or particular reader demographic, or a particular genre and reader demographic, Elizabeth Long examines reading within a specific cultural formation: the book club. In *Book Clubs: Women and the Uses of Reading in Everyday Life* (2003), Long brings to the foreground the overtly social nature of reading, in order to challenge what she calls the ideology of the solitary reader, an ideology that 'governs our understanding of reading' (Long 2003:3). This powerful ideology has suppressed, and continues to suppress 'the ways in which reading is socially framed' (Long 2003:11). Once this ideology is disturbed then the truly social nature of reading, its 'various prospects, linkages, and relationships within the sociocultural world can be visible' (Long 2003:17).

In her ethnographic work, Long examines reading groups populated by white college-educated women, groups that she presupposed would function as a stage for the acting out of an individual reader's interpretation of a particular book. However, in another example of ethnography's ability to surprise its acolytes, Long argues that, unlike professional readers, discussions moved quickly and unexpectedly beyond textual interpretation as members shared more intimate understandings of their readings. The discussions 'move back and forth between using people's remarks as windows into the texts (the primary imperative of literary analysis) and using the text as a window into people's lives or various aspects of the cultural and social lives we live together' (Long 2003:145). So, even though books as texts are still significant they are also thoroughly contextualised through the creative actions of the reading groups. Central to the function of book clubs is an 'intersubjective accomplishment' that 'enable[s] participants to articulate or even discover who they are: their values, their aspirations, and their stance toward the dilemmas of their world' (ibid.). Books clubs, when conceptualised in this way, take their place as an element within civil society. By demonstrating the function of books and reading within a particular reading community, the common perception that reading is an individual, private and solitary activity is severely tested.

Long concentrates on reading as it is manifest within a semi-formal cultural formation. The structure of the book club, with its office bearers and regular meeting places and times, is of great help to ethnographers because, unlike a study of more dispersed reading subjects, the membership of the book club has a material presence—the researcher can watch and listen to a book club in operation. It is one of the few occasions when conventional participant observation is applicable to the study of reading. However, I would argue that, as most everyday reading does not occur within the structure of a book club or reading group, uncritically transferring the meanings and uses of books within book clubs to everyday readers in general may not be appropriate. Recognition of the often dispersed nature of recreational reading, however, should not be mistaken as a counter-reformation to reinstate the ideology of the solitary reader: solitary they may often be but asocial they are not.

Everyday readers: readers and methods

Having provided an overview of ethnography and its use in the study of popular reading, I would like to now move away from such historical and theoretical concerns toward something more concrete: the ethnographic methodology of this particular work.

The readers

The most important element of any ethnographic study is the cultural actors themselves; without finding people prepared to give their time and share their views and opinions, ethnographic work would be impossible. From the outset, ethnographers place their trust in their collaborators. Contacting people who are willing to take part in a study is often a difficult task. To this end, I placed notices on various on-line list-servers, at local public libraries and on noticeboards around the University of New South Wales campus. Notices were also given to friends, acquaintances and colleagues who, in turn, circulated them in other places. The most effective way of enlisting the aid of informants was, however, via 'word-of-mouth' or 'snowballing'. As a result of the 'snowballing' technique, some of the readers came to the interview having been told what to expect. Therefore, some participants were forewarned of the topic areas and even of specific questions they would be asked. This no doubt contributed to the degree of class and gender homogeneity among the readers I interviewed. This having been said, it is important to be aware that while the readers may appear similar, such gender and class similarities do not, automatically, translate to similarities in all aspects of their reading practice (Moss 1993:133). These instances provide support for the maintenance a degree of distinction between the social and the cultural.

Of the 21 readers interviewed for this study, only four were men. This follows almost all research undertaken into fiction reading; women read more fiction, of all kinds, than their male counterparts. The readers' educational backgrounds, in the formal sense, were similar. All the readers, bar one, had completed their secondary schooling, some in private and others in state high schools. With a single exception, all had university degrees or were engaged in some form of tertiary education. Two readers actually had postgraduate qualifications in the humanities. Although their age-range varied between 20 and 51 years of age, most of the readers were located within the 20 to 35 age bracket. At the time of the interview most of the readers were living in the generally affluent eastern or gentrified inner-western suburbs of Sydney, although some had previously lived in other areas of the city, other states of Australia, or even overseas. All the readers were employed in either white-collar or service industry occupations. Those in service industries were mostly students funding their education with casual employment. The ethnic backgrounds of the readers were overwhelmingly English-speaking.

The research method: semi-formal interview

Although I set out to study everyday reading practices, it could be argued that there is nothing 'everyday' about an ethnographic interview, and that informants in such circumstances are always placed immediately into 'artificial situations' (Hammersley cited in Wilson 1992:112). Rather than see the interview as artificial, it may be more productive to regard the exchange between interviewee and interviewee as, itself, a social situation in which the subject is interacting, creatively, with both the researcher and the anticipated audience for their opinions and views (Tonkin 1992:39). To suggest that being interviewed is a totally alien or artificial experience is to deny the amount of informal or unconscious ethnographic work that exists outside academic initiatives. By informal ethnographic work I mean the production of those accounts of cultural experiences that people do all the time. The recounting of a weekend's activities to a friend, answering questions asked by a telemarketer and the post-cinema film discussion are all instances of informal ethnographic work: 'we are, it seems, *homo narrans*: humankind the narrators and story tellers' (Plummer 1995:5). In comparison to these informal works, the formal academic project is a conscious and pragmatic 'bracketing' of the common act of self-representation. Therefore, far from being a completely foreign experience, and the power relations inherent in the ethnographic interview notwithstanding, people are experienced in making self-representations, conscious or otherwise, to others for various purposes.

The readers were interviewed semi-formally.[4] Interviews were between 25 minutes and three hours in duration, the length determined by the interviewees' willingness to speak about their cultural lives. It is tempting to claim that these interviews were unstructured but despite the naturalistic claims of some research projects, all methods of interviewing entail some degree of structure (Wilson 1992:96). Moreover, informants as well as researchers contribute to the interview's organisation (Hammersley and Atkinson 1983:112-113). The readers were encouraged to ask questions about me, the research and their role, which they often did. Most of the interviews began slowly, the interviewees were often nervous; however, this would change during the course of the discussion. Apart from a few exceptions, all the readers who contributed to this study did so with great enthusiasm and seemed to enjoy talking about their reading. As I later discovered, talking about books was already part of their reading culture.

Conclusion

In referring to everyday rather than popular reading this book tries to avoid the seemingly endless definitional problems that are always faced when the word 'popular' is used to describe particular modes of cultural consumption. Along with 'the popular', textual analysis is also jettisoned in favour of an ethnographic approach that is more sensitive to everyday reading practices. Despite a profusion of theoretical and methodological discourse that surrounds ethnographic work, ethnography nonetheless remains a fundamentally pragmatic form of research that tries to see cultural practices from the position of cultural actors themselves. But in trying see everyday reading from the viewpoint of everyday readers this book comes up against the problems faced by all such research. This empathetic aim of ethnographic and qualitative methods is far from infallible because 'the people we study often do not give stable or consistent meanings to things, people and events' (Becker

1996:3) and I would add perhaps not to their readings of particular books either. 'They change their minds frequently,' Becker continues, and 'worse yet, they are often not sure what things do mean; they make vague and woolly interpretations of events and people. ... we ought to respect that confusion and inability to be decisive by not giving things a more stable meaning than the people involved do.' This fluidity in interpretation comes at a cost to the researcher 'since it is hard to describe, let alone measure, such a moving target' (ibid.). Therefore, any ethnographic study of everyday reading brings a degree of order and cohesion to people's cultural activities that may not be there, in a wholly conscious sense, in the process of daily living: as the narrator of Sartre's *Nausea* suggests: 'when you tell about a life, everything changes' (Sartre 1981:62): narrating culture is never the same as living culture; talking about reading a book is not the same as reading a book. In ethnographic cultural accounts the cohesion afforded by narrative is not just an imposition of the academic 'I' however. In this book, the readers narrate their experiences to the researcher who, in turn, then uses the readers' narratives to produce cultural accounts. It is with these caveats in mind that the following discussion, which begins with the cultural geography of everyday reading, needs to be read.

Notes

1. There was a 'democratic impulse motivating researchers whose aim was to document "hidden lives" and worlds, to tell different stories and reveal different accounts' (Gray 1997:92).
2. William Shaffir (1999) suggests soberly that 'little is gained by being doctrinaire about how ethnographic research should be accomplished' (Shaffir 1999:685). Likewise, Hobbs and May (1993) argue that ethnography is a diverse collection of practices, 'there is no such thing as methodological purity' (Hobbs and May 1993:viii).
3. See Johnson (1998) and Nightingale (1996) for a detailed discussion of this binary.
4. Further details about the interviews and the interview questions may be found in Appendix B.

2 'I Can Read at Any Time, but I Can't Read Anywhere': The Place of Everyday Reading

One can transform a place by reading in it.
Alberto Manguel, A History of Reading

There are passages of Ulysses which can be read only in the toilet—if one wants to extract the full flavour of their content.
Henry Miller, The Books in My Life

Introduction

Reading as a cultural activity highlights the seemingly paradoxical nature of culture. On an experiential level, reading is an intimate and individual pursuit, often undertaken in silence. Yet simultaneously, reading is always a collective and social act in that individual readers rely on materials—the skills for reading, access to books and the time for reading—that are derived socially. All these materials require some form of capital; all need to be acquired before reading can take place. Even Harold Bloom, the arch-defender of the aesthetic against the social, is willing to concede that the solitary meditation required to read correctly 'must be purchased from the community' (Bloom 1994:23). One such purchase that all readers must make is that of the time and space in which read. While everyday reading may appear to be free of the strictures that confine and inhibit professional readers, it would be quite wrong to think that it is entirely formless or chaotic because it remains subject to cultural economies of time and space. Within such a spatio-temporal economy readers have to create a *place* for reading which, unlike professional readers, is never a given. Such considerations are significant because 'culture, however defined, can only be approached as embedded in real-life situations, in temporally and spatially specific ways' (Crang 1998:1). It is to this cultural geography of everyday reading that this chapter is devoted.

Disorderly reading?

The simple, commonplace word 'reading' denotes a wide range of historically variable socio-cultural practices. The early order of reading of the late-medieval and early-modern periods required not only the reading of particular canonical texts but also 'specific rituals for the readers' behaviour and for the use of books that require environments with special furnishing and instruments' (Petrucci 1999:363). Reading was regulated in terms of not only the texts to be read, but also the spaces in which reading was to be performed: particular books were to be read in particular ways, in particular surroundings. The rituals that contributed to such practices did much, along with the scarcity and therefore expense of texts, to sacralise books and book-reading (Spender 1995:45). Consequently, changes to the rituals of reading contribute to a change in the cultural and social status of books.

The regulated practices of professional and scholarly reading have always been in conflict with the less professionally and commercially regimented reading activities of others. These vernacular reading practices have drawn various responses from those whose cultural power derives from the operation of the dominant order: toleration, derision, prohibition or appropriation. Raymond Williams suggests that the emergence of a reading public, however attenuated, coincides with the appearance of the now familiar assertions of cultural decline from those with cultural authority (Williams 1961:179). In the twentieth and twenty-first centuries, highly ordered practices of reading still operate in the academy—close reading for example—and within other knowledge-producing institutions like the law. But reading has become an increasingly unruly activity under the conditions of modernity and the amount of reading conducted outside, or at a distance from aesthetic, professional and scholarly institutions, has increased with the size of the reading public and the quantity of books produced. Historian of the book, Antonio Petrucci, finds the most salient challenges to ordered reading practices in the reading culture of the young who, he claims, 'represent a public that rejects the canon—any canon—and prefers anarchical choices' (Petrucci 1999:364).

Mobile readers

A major catalyst for these anarchic choices is the breakdown in the normative modes of reading. Contemporary readers are more likely to make the book fit their bodies and the social spaces through which they move. Indeed, the paperback book was designed to accompany an increasingly mobile readership (Schrevders 1981:5). For a reader like Dirk, books and reading are the accompaniment to the activities and demands of his everyday life:

> if I'm reading something I'll read it while I'm cleaning my teeth, I'll read it while
> I'm eating my breakfast, I'll read while I'm walking to the train station, I'll read
> while I'm sitting at traffic-lights in my car, I'll read anywhere (D).

Madelaine too seems prepared to read in a wide range of places, and it would appear, at any time:

> I read everywhere, in bed before I sleep. At the kitchen table while I am
> cooking meals. In the train, if I can get a seat. While having lunch at work, if I
> am alone. I don't read if I am sharing meals with people, too antisocial. I
> would actually prefer to read than to talk but would not be so impolite (M).

Readers carry books in their pockets or bags to be read on a train or in a lunch-hour; the size of coat pockets actually helped determine the physical dimensions of the paperback (Schrevders 1981:8). Thoroughly de-sacralised, books are taken on holiday, read on the beach, in bed, and even in the bath; toilet-reading seems, anecdotally at least, to be a not uncommon cultural activity: two readers told me that they stack reading material next to the toilet.[1] One reader even read while exerting herself on an exercise bike:

> *So, do you read anywhere else?*
> Yes, on my exercise bike, which is sort of stupid but I made a pact to do half-
> an-hour a day on an exercise bike and if I read it takes my mind off how much
> it hurts and how uncomfortable I am [laughs] so I read then too (F).

Frances, a 27-year-old administrative manager, comments here on the transformative power of reading: the ability of reading to change a reader's consciousness of a particular space, and even of his or her own body.

The increased intimacy between book and reader cannot but affect reading habits (Petrucci 1999:365). It is this increasingly intimate, rather than externally regimented, relationship that has contributed to reading becoming a less disciplined act; individuals appear to be reading what they want, where they want and taking from their books the meanings and pleasures that they want. But while the possibility for truly anarchic reading modes may exist, such a view seems to overlook the constraints that limit and shape reading practices. Reading a dog-eared, broken-spined copy of a paperback on a bus may seem anarchic when compared to the highly stratified and restricted reading practices of a medieval scholar, but such seemingly unfettered reading practices nonetheless operate within discernible confines. Rather than displaying an anarchic imperative, the readers I interviewed appear to read within quite specific parameters. The availability of the time and space of reading is one such parameter. The spatio-temporal economy of everyday reading differs from those of professional and institutional readers whose reading practices have exchange value and, therefore, an allotted place within commodity relations.

The spatio-temporal economy of everyday reading

In his study of the phenomenology of the personal stereo, *Sounding Out the City* (2000), Michael Bull argues that time is 'the dominant contingency of everyday life' (Bull 2000:55). Bull contrasts two sorts of time: the cyclical and the rational. Cyclical time refers to 'natural time': the passing of the seasons, the transition from night to day, and the biological time of the body. Rational time, in contrast, is an abstract measure superimposed over diurnal and seasonal time (Bull 2000:67); it is time objectified through technologies such as the clock, the calendar and the timetable. The movement from cyclical to linear conceptions of time marks a change in human consciousness that is constitutive of the conditions or perhaps even one of the preconditions of modernity (Berman 1983; Giddens 1990).

The development of communications media has made a significant contribution to such alterations to the substance of social life, temporal and spatial (Thompson 1995:31). Under these changed and changing living conditions, the naturalised 'technologies of time' have become integral to the means of production because people's apprehension of 'time is increasingly linked to the time-keeping mechanism required for the synchronisation of labour and the organisation of the working week' (Thompson 1995:36). As well as a contingency then, time may also be regarded a commodity and a valuable one at that. Max Weber outlined that under the Protestant work ethic a 'waste of time is thus the first and in principle the deadliest sin ... Loss of time through sociability, idle talk, luxury, even more sleep than is necessary to health ... is worthy of absolute moral condemnation' (Weber 1930:157). Phrases like 'spending time' or 'wasting time' lose their metaphorical status when time is thought of in this fashion. Moreover, such rationalised temporal regimes operate as a mechanism of social control: people are not just orientated '*to* time, they are disciplined *by* time (Urry 1995:5, original emphasis). In addition to being conceptualised as a contingency and a commodity, time should therefore also be thought of as power. Time is not objectively real—a universal phenomenon—but neither is it romantically subjective. Rather, time is fashioned as a cultural object and 'internalised as part of self' (Rutz 1992:3). As a consequence, time becomes a site of cultural and political conflict. Particular uses of time are instances of cultural agency in that 'agents place particular constructions on time, and time becomes objectified in "interested" and "intentional" ways' (ibid.). Reading is one way in which this interested and intentional objectification of time is revealed; 'consumer culture as the personal organization of time is one way into the ethnography of popular aesthetics' (Inglis 1988:87).

Time to read

The *Books Alive* survey found that 'among those who had read for pleasure ... there was wide variation in the time spent, but the average time spent reading over the week was 8.1 hours' (*Books Alive* 2001:7). In comparison, the average weekly reading time of my readers was almost identical, 8.2 hours per week. However, this mean masks the asymmetry in reading times manifest within the group: three readers found or manufactured over twenty hours for recreational reading, while another could spare only two. Almost all the readers told me that they did not have as much time to read as they would like and for readers like Frances, time was the main constraint on their reading. Her normal rate of book reading would be 'probably six a month,' (F) but when she has more free time her reading increases significantly:

> *If you had more time do you think you would read more?*
> Yes.
> *Time is the major limit?*
> Yes, definitely, like when I was on holidays I read during the days and so I would be reading a book a day pretty much, which was lovely but depends on the book, some days it was just too hot to do anything so we were just lazing around reading books (F).

Frances's reading increases markedly during her holidays: from six books per month to one book a day. In the above excerpt, holiday reading is represented as something rather decadent, something to do while 'lazing around', free from the strictures of one's normal routine. This aspect of reading is also expressed by Natasha who, while on vacation, read 'a whole stack of good books like *The Shipping News* ' (N). In this situation reading acquires an almost pastoral complexion. In fact, for Roz, reading 'outside time'—which is akin to Frances's and Natasha's holiday reading—appears to be an almost utopian state: 'if I had the time I'd read a whole book in a day and finish it in a day' (R). The appeal of reading 'outside time' is noted by Meredith Rogers Cherland in her American study of teenage girls' literary practices. One reader told the interviewer that 'reading without worrying about time was a real pleasure' (Cherland 1994:174).

On one level, comments about insufficient reading time could be an attempt to impress the interviewer, an apparently middle-class male academic asking questions about the nature of their reading culture. When presenting oneself to others, an individual will 'tend to incorporate and exemplify the officially accredited values of the society, more so, in fact, than does his [or her] behaviour as a whole' (Goffman 1959:45). Operating under a 'curve of deference', the interviewees may therefore want to appear more committed to a particular cultural activity than is really the case (Rowse 1985: 42-43). The problem with these 'deferential' opinions is that they 'may hide

real and deep-rooted adherence to alternative traditions of cultural preference' (Rowse 1985:43). Comments about a lack of reading time could be
interpreted as deferential in tone, but equally these views could be aspirational
statements based firmly in the rhetoric of class-inflected cultural values. All
the readers I interviewed came from middle-class backgrounds where reading is most likely to be tacitly, if not expressly, encouraged and valued: reading is good, reading more is better. Recreational reading is important to these
readers, so their claimed lack of reading opportunities, its ideological or deferential origins aside, is likely to be a genuine concern.

The availability of reading time affects not only the total of amount of
reading undertaken, but also a reader's choice of book and his or her style of
reading. For example, Georgina spoke of almost buying Martin Amis's *London Fields*: 'I read the first page and I thought oh, I can see myself wanting
to read this all the time, I've got too much on this week, it's too long, I'll
leave it til next week' (G). In a similar vein, Dirk blames a lack of time for his
friends' inability to read the books he lends them: 'I think that's because, a
lot of the stuff [the books he lends], people can't give it the time to, to fully
appreciate it, like some of the stuff, I mean Robert Jordan stuff, it's very
long, you're talking a minimum of 800 pages, that's a lot of reading to do'
(D). As well as influencing the total amount of reading and the selection of
particular texts, the availability of reading time may also contribute to some
readers' 'extensive' reading. Natasha spoke about her reading style which
seemed to be influenced, somewhat counter-intuitively by a lack of reading
opportunities: 'I guess it's an economy of reading, I don't have a lot of time
to read so I'm not gunna read something twice' (N). In speaking of an
'economy of reading', Natasha here suggests that reading time is a scarce
commodity. An awareness of a temporal reading economy is also expressed
by Winston who, like Natasha, casts re-reading books as a luxury he cannot
afford:

> I have but I don't do it a lot [...] I think because there is too much to read, I
> mean but, I want to re-read *Crime and Punishment* and I just don't think I will
> because there is so much other stuff to read (W).

Likewise, time was a major influence on Eric's book choice: 'once again I
only have so much time, so I'm constantly thinking how best to fill in my
time with the appropriate, the appropriate works I suppose' (E). Asked if
time was significant he continued: 'yes definitely, definitely [...] there are so
many books to be read and so little time to read them' (E). When choosing a
book, therefore, he is 'always looking for checks and balances, I suppose to
make certain I'm reading something that is worthwhile, so that I'm not going
to waste my time' (E). Interestingly though, Eric was also a frequent *re-reader*

so it is not possible to state, categorically, that a scarcity of reading time (or a wider selection of books) will always produce an extensive reading mode.

Restrictions on reading time impact seriously upon reading practices. In the following interview extract, Georgina outlines her everyday reading style in which time is a crucial, if not determining, consideration:

> I normally have sort of three different books I'm trying to read at the same time, if I get them all read finished well that's another question but they [the books] will normally travel around with me if I've got a spare minute or you know waiting for the bus or waiting for someone if you're waiting to meet someone I get one of them [books] out, I'm normally reading three things at the same time.
>
> *You use the time as it presents itself?*
> Yes if you, if you've got 20 minutes spare during the day you sort of grab that and use that. I'm not too structured in when I'm gonna read something, just kind of like when the opportunity presents itself I can (G).

Significantly, Georgina expresses three distinct conceptions of time: as a commodity ('if I've got a spare minute'); as a contingency (reading 'when the opportunity presents itself'); and as an object ('if you've got 20 minutes during the day you sort of grab it'). Georgina reads in a fragmented way because that is all time allows. Reading fills the cracks in the day, both those expected and those that are contingent. She carries books with her in order that she may take the opportunity should it arise. The contingency of reading time is also mentioned by Lana who, when asked if she put time aside for reading, replies: 'I don't actually put it aside, I take it as it comes' (L). In addition to 'going prepared' to read, readers also borrow time normally allocated to other commitments, 'you can include it [reading] in other activities, if you're going somewhere you can read it on the train, or in the car, whatever you do, read it in class [laughs]' (D). Apparently, some readers are even prepared to borrow time from sleep: 'I used to get up early and read before I came here [to university], but I stopped doing that because it was just too tiring' (W)—as with all things borrowed, time has to be returned. Martyn Lyons (1992) describes this fragmented mode of reading engendered by living in a modern industrialised society:

> the regulated working day allows only short fragments of reading time, which must be seized in the interstices between home and work, between work and sleep, in lunch breaks, on commuter trains, between the electric iron and the vacuum cleaner (Lyons 1992:6).

Modern everyday reading styles are not so much anarchic or chaotic, as episodic (Lyons 1992).[2] Georgina's reading order, like all the readers I spoke to, is far from chaotic. Contrary to Petrucci (1999), she and they are not free to read when and where they wish, a fact of which my readers seem acutely aware, hence the lengths to which they are prepared to go in order to make a time for their books. Episodic reading requires the conscious organisation of reading time.

Reading in social spaces

The time of reading cannot exist without a place in which to read. The place in which reading occurs is a constitutive element in the order of reading. Naomi Baron has argued that: '[w]here we read (or read to) is often an indication of social attitudes and practical access to written materials' (Baron 2000:85). It is a surprise then that cultural studies approaches to text—with its concentration, even fixation on the relationship between power and culture—seem to have largely neglected the question of where reading actually takes place. In subcultural, television and popular music studies the physical space of the cultural performance is deemed to be highly significant, but the space of reading is often relegated or omitted completely.[3] One of the strengths of Radway's classic study (1984) was the way it examined reading as a spatially constituted act: an act performed within both a particular reading community and an individual's home.

Inadequate appraisal of the space of reading does much to confirm the assumption that reading is a purely private, self-contained affair. As a result, reading for pleasure becomes associated with the domestic sphere, which, in turn, casts reading as a passive cultural act without a public presence. Cultural and literary critics have gone to some lengths to stress the active nature of reading, as it is possible to regard reading as but one step removed from doing nothing.[4] As de Certeau writes—auditioning for the role of devil's advocate—reading 'seems to constitute the maximal development of the passivity assumed to characterize the consumer' (de Certeau 1984:xxi). The important word here is 'assumed'. The assumption that reading is a passive activity also helps maintain the belief that reading fiction is a feminised cultural activity. Much of the research undertaken in this area seems to confirm this perception; fiction reading is more likely to be practised by women than men. Indeed, some research suggests that gender is the most important single factor affecting reading activity (Bennett *et al.* 1999:148).

The existence of gendered spheres of reading is confirmed by some of the women readers in my study, who make a similar contrast between their reading and the reading of male partners and friends. Julie, who is a university administrator, highlighted the difference between her reading and that of her husband: 'he's read only one novel in his life, I think he thinks it's a waste of time' (J). Her husband's preference is for historical and philosophical books: in his opinion, Julie explained, 'why would you read a novel when you can read *The Crucible of Consciousness* or Karl Jung's collected works eh?' (J). Rather than see this difference as one of socialisation, she frames it in terms of ontological properties: 'I don't think he has a strong imaginative world which I think a lot of probably a lot of people who like to read [fiction] do' (J). Madelaine, a woman of the same generation as Julie (they are both in their fifties), made the same implied value judgement of her male partner's reading: 'he is not a reader, only technical magazines, yuk' (M). Reading technical magazines, from Madelaine's perspective, barely qualifies as reading at all: reading is code for 'reading fiction'. Like Julie, Madelaine relies on a biological and essentialist, not socio-cultural, explanation for gender-based reading differences: 'he is very left brain and I am very right brain' (M). This disparity is also inter-generational. Lana, who is 24, reported that she and her male partner had 'done a bit of reading together but mostly me reading a book and him reading how to program Java, and *Secrets of Aquatic Chemistry* and other exciting things' (L). Again here the tone is dismissive, a little sarcastic, and even conspiratorial: Lana expected me to agree with her dismissal of science textbooks as less than interesting.

The dearth of fiction reading in men is not an issue with which my study engages directly. Aside from the opinions of female interviewers regarding the nature of their male partners' and friends' reading habits, the men that I have interviewed are, for obvious reasons, fiction readers. Men's preference for reading non-fiction—history books, auto/biography and professional and hobby related texts (Guldberg 1990; Bennett *et al.* 1999)—may counter the accusations of passivity with their implicit promise of future action; the useful reading of guides to Java programming or golf magazines are validated by the possibility of material action, and the promise of more effective action, in the future. The reading of fiction, in contrast, appears to offer no such direct promise of social agency. Fiction reading is not an avenue to power: 'reading fiction may develop all kinds of personal skills and understanding,' hard currency in the private sphere, but not 'marketable qualities' in the public domain (McKernan 1990:87). In fact, reading fiction is often regarded as a form of passive recreation that constitutes a retreat from the public sphere, the site of privileged social, cultural and political action. Such a belief is an obvious denial of the co-dependent nature of the public and private and the role of the private sphere in cultural production and reproduction. Batsleer *et al.* (1985) suggest that the significance of a cultural activity like reading that occurs 'in an unorganised and almost unnoticed way in thousands of homes and workplaces everyday', and as detached from the social world as it may at first seem, might be as politically and ideologically 'effectual as those produced in the class room or the street' (Batsleer *et al.* 1985:155). McKenzie Wark goes as far to suggest that 'acts of reading that take place with the telly on in the suburban living room', and other types of media consumption, 'are what constitute the actual public culture of the nation. It might not be the ideal "public sphere" imagined by political theorists, but unlike the latter, it actually exists' (Wark 1999:134).

The yoking of reading and watching television as domestic and similarly passive cultural phenomena is challenged by many of my interviewees who see reading and watching television as dissimilar activities.[5] For Eric, there is a significant difference between reading and television. He claims to not watch much television, but his partner, a nurse, is an avid viewer in her 'off time':

> she's quite happy to squander her off time, or what I would say is squander her time away from work and I find that irritating, that I think she should be doing something productive and once again I guess it's arrogance but I, I don't see as being productive, while reading I do see as productive, reading is more productive than watching television.
>
> *Do you actually talk about this?*
> Yeah, yeah, it's kind of broached humorously and often digresses into something else (E).

Eric's partner's television viewing is wasteful, whereas the hours he spends reading are 'productive'. Such sentiments are echoed by Karen, a 30-year-old psychologist, who stated quite clearly the differences she perceived between watching television and reading a book:

> it's more interesting [reading] I mean, TV is easier isn't it? And if I'm really tired [after a day's work] I fall into the trap I think of watching too much TV. So I kinda have to be, I have to be quite strict with myself sometimes not to do that coz I know that number one, I don't get the same amount of satisfaction out of it, so reading is something that you can do where you do get, you know it's active, you do get some kind of satisfaction out of it, you're immersed in it, it's a complete distraction from anything that you're thinking before hand because you have to, you have to kind of be active in it (K).

According to Karen, the active nature of reading—as she perceives it—sets book-reading at odds with television-viewing. There is also a sense in which watching television is an 'easy' activity, one that requires less involvement than reading a printed page. Karen's comment advances the modernist view that visual entertainment is an all too easy and dangerous pleasure; the rewards of reading are superior because readers have to work harder than television or cinema viewers to gain their entertainment. Later in the interview Karen told me that 'when I get quite stressed out at work then we can often get to the stage where we put it on, the TV, when we get home, it's a hard habit to get out of' (K). Television is presented as a habit and, like most habits, it is something negative and an activity to be avoided: 'I have to be quite strict with myself sometimes' (K). Yet while reading is also a life-time habit for this particular reader, she does not describe her many hours spent reading in the same terms.

Karen's comments also highlight the relationship between work and leisure. Just as a hard shift in a factory or the call-centre may not leave enough energy for reading in the evening so, after a day's professional practice, in a profession that requires much careful reading, coming home to a complex novel may not constitute a clear enough break between work and leisure activities. As a teenager, she used to read 'classics' but not now:

> I'd find it [a classical novel] too heavy, like I think especially because I read for work, so I read papers and I read books to do with work, so when I'm not reading those things what I want to do is read for entertainment and so, I'd read thrillers kind of things, like science fiction, fantasy kind of things, detective novels and contemporary novels as well (K).

Reading for 'entertainment' leads this reader to avoid 'heavy' books in favour of genre and 'contemporary novels'. The choice of text is guided by the intended purpose of reading within a particular time and space. Karen's conception of leisure as time away from work is a common-place model; leisure time is the free time purchased through labour within capitalist relations of production (Lefebvre 1991:40). But to conceptualise leisure as the other of paid work is to define leisure in very androcentric terms. Such a masculinist model of the relationship between work and 'free-time' denies the gendered nature of domestic space and the amount of unpaid work that woman undertake in that environment: home for many women is not a place away from work but another workplace (McDowell and Pringle 1992:131). By perceiving leisure as 'grace after the meal' (Williams 1965:132), Karen frames her leisure in masculinist terms. This may be facilitated by her employment within a profession and her lack of conventional family responsibilities, like children.

Just as Karen's recreational reading is influenced by her mentally exhausting professional practice, so Catarina's everyday reading is affected by her university studies. Here she talks about reading for recreation while under pressure to read and write for university assignments:

> *What sort of things do you like reading now?*
> at the moment something that is really, really simple, like not complex, not difficult to understand at all, I've got a really short attention span at the moment, so I'm reading the newspaper for the first time in a very long time well, still I'm finding it really hard to finish anything so it took me, the last thing I read all the way through was that Billy Connolly book [*Billy*] and that was really bad and I kept on reading it anyway, it took me a really long time to do it and *High Fidelity* which I really liked (C).

She then juxtaposes reading something 'really simple' in short bursts with a more sustained academic reading practice:

> I like reading something just because I could, I didn't have to highlight anything, it didn't matter whether I agreed with it or not, or if I got it or not, I didn't have to take notes on it, so I just like reading bits and pieces, it's a bit of a commitment to get a book (C).

These comments make it very difficult to crudely read the cultural and the social from the textual: putatively 'simple' texts are too often equated with an allegedly 'simple' readership. As Raymond Williams realised over fifty years ago, there is a real possibility for self-delusion if highly literate people—including critics, researchers and scholars—suppose that they 'can judge the quality of general living by primary reference to the reading artifacts' (Williams 1958:209). The failure to read classical novels is not one of ability, or opportunity, but purpose: Karen cannot make 'classical novels' mean in the way, and at the time, she requires. In Catarina's case, reading simple books is a break from the complex reading demanded by a university programme. Reading uncomplicated texts in a desultory manner contrasts with the 'commitment' of reading a 'serious' novel, a commitment that this reader cannot always undertake. The extent to which a particular text may be accommodated within everyday obligations and routines is a defining characteristic of every day media use (Hermes 1995:64).

Reading and silence

Apart from its association with domestic space and its status as a stereotypically feminine cultural activity, the representation of reading as a passive cultural pursuit may also spring from its predominantly silent execution. Reading in silence has its modern origin in the monastic scriptoria of the late Middle Ages before it colonised schools, universities and the lay aristocracy by the fourteenth century (Chartier 1995:16). Arising from the pedagogical practices of the early modern period, silent reading becomes an integral part of the dominant order of reading as it was practised in the bourgeois schools of the nineteenth and twentieth centuries (Petrucci 1999; Baron 2000). From this institutional base, silent reading is offered as an optimal and normative reading practice.

In order to read in silence the reader needs to have access to a place away from others. In this sense, like time, silence becomes a cultural commodity that needs to be acquired before 'correct' reading may occur, a commodity that is purchased via the private control of space. People without access to such physical spaces were not, and are not, able to read in this way (Vincent 2000:102). George Steiner indicates how an 'economics of space and of leisure' has been crucial to the development of particular normative reading practices; a classical act of reading has always been reliant on 'the private ownership of space, of silence, and of books themselves,' a practice that, 'never represented a natural or native formula' (Steiner 1988:41). The point, however, is that this order of reading *has* come to represent the only legitimate way to engage with a text.[6]

In my interviews, readers often suggested that reading silently was their preferred mode: 'I like to be in a room on my own, I'm not keen to read with other people' (J); 'I can't stand having the music on or anything, I hate that, I hate having music on when I'm reading' (F); and 'I can read with music but I prefer to read in silence' (V) are frequent comments. Moreover, reading in silence is necessary for some of the informants' full, proper, or correct appreciation of the book. Reading in the presence of music is, for this reader, rather arduous:

> well I can't read, some people go to sleep with music going but I don't because I stay awake to listen to it, the sound, I think I listen too much, yeah quite often there will be people in the other room, may have music on or the TV or something, that doesn't bother me, but if people are talking it doesn't effect me, but in the actual room that I'm in, I find it very difficult to concentrate with music going mainly because I start listening to the song or the DJ or whatever and then I just suddenly realise that I've scanned down the page without taking anything in (M).

Ideally, reading in silence requires a space devoted to nothing but reading. Lana needs a peaceful reading environment, and so likes to read when her flat-mate is not home, when she 'can get access to a quiet space', access to a space that is really a temporary place of her own creation (L).

Many readers live in the limited space of an apartment, space most often shared with other people. As Stephen Riggins notes, the living room or lounge 'constitutes a transactional space for the household' (Riggins 1994:101). Furthermore, households and the social relationships within them are 'microsocial environments' that facilitate and constrain cultural practices (Morley and Silverstone 1990:32-33). For reading to be practised within the home, but outside the bedroom, it must occur within a space used for other cultural activities, notably listening to music, watching television, eating, and cooking. If music is sometimes tolerable, especially varieties without lyrics, then reading with the television on seems to be a serious distraction: 'I often read with music playing. But I could never read whilst also watching TV. I can't read and also concentrate on other stimuli' (M). Similarly, Eric believed that he could not read effectively in a room where a television is playing: 'I can't be in the same room, with the TV because I'll watch the TV or I'll be trying to do both and I'll do neither' (E). Eric's girlfriend, in his opinion, watches an excessive amount of television, an activity that interferes with his reading:

Outside your bedroom, do you read in the company of others?
Yeah, I live in a small flat with my girlfriend so I guess she's there most of the time. [...] she watches too much television and well, to my mind she watches too much television, and I tend to sort of sit in front of the TV rather than read sometimes, I think, this is crap I should be reading (E).

The multiple use of domestic space has to be negotiated by Karen whose partner also watches television while she is reading: '[t]he other day he was watching television it was very annoying, he kept flicking channels' (K). Ivana too is interrupted by her non-reading boyfriend: he 'bugs me, [laughs] he makes a lot of noise [laughs]' when 'he needs attention' (I). Likewise, Anthony finds it 'far too distracting' to read in the living room while his partner is watching the television, so he usually reads in his bedroom; he manages the competing demands on limited domestic space by retreating to another room (A). As a result, reading can become an anti-social activity as it can require a degree of withdrawal, physical and psychological, from those around the reader (Meyrowitz 1988:143):

> my poor husband often has long conversations with himself because, whilst reading, I have turned off all external sound, including his voice. When my children were little, they knew that they could pretty well say and do what they liked once I became immersed in a book, scary eh?
> [...]
> I am conscious that reading can be anti-social so I read most when alone (M).

The time and space for reading have, therefore, to be negotiated with the other occupants of the domestic space. These negotiations, according to the interviewees' stories, seem to be unequal in that reading does not impinge upon another person's television viewing, but the opposite is often the case. Logically, those readers who can read undisturbed by the activities of others occupying the same domestic space find more opportunity to read within the common areas of the home. To this end, some readers are able to read in what may seem to be, when compared to the stipulations of the normative reading order, the most unfavourable surroundings:

> *You can sit in the lounge room with other people and read?*
> Yes, with the TV on, yes.
>
> *It doesn't cause distractions?*
> depends what I'm reading sometimes, sometimes I'll get up and stop, but I couldn't sit there in front of something I really wanted to watch and read because then I want to watch it, but sometimes I just like being with people not necessarily having to talk to them, but just be in a room where there's someone else, and if that means there's other noise going on then I just block it out, it's no big deal (C).

Roz, too, has developed an ability to read amidst shared cultural spaces, and would probably agree with Catarina that reading surrounded by others is 'no big deal':

When you read, do you have to read in silence?
No, no I can read in crowded trains with people yelling, I can read [while sitting] backwards on buses which not many people can do, it doesn't really matter I've been trained now.

So, can you read with the TV on?
I tend to get distracted though I must admit, I tend to read during the commercials [laughs] and then I'll go back to watching the show if I'm interested.

You fit a lot of reading into a day?
Yeah, heaps, an unbelievable amount I think (R).

Roz has 'been trained now'—she has trained herself—to read surrounded by distractions. This training seems to facilitate an amount of reading that would probably be impossible if she only read normatively, in solitude and in silence.

Spaces of reading: the bedroom

If readers cannot adequately negotiate a place of reading within the shared domestic space of the home, then reading in their bedroom becomes a significant cultural activity. Researchers have outlined the importance of the 'culture of the bedroom' in the cultural practices of adolescents (McRobbie and Garber 1976; Baker 2001). Bedrooms provide a space within the home in which young people may engage in cultural practices out of the direct gaze of their family; the bedroom is a site of relative cultural autonomy. The important role of 'bedroom culture' seems to continue in later life. The bedroom is a space within which cultural actors may engage in particular cultural activities that constitute the ownership of that particular span of time as leisure (Inglis 1988:85). For example, bedroom reading has been, historically, part of the reading practices of Australia working-class readers (Lyons 2001). For Buckridge, Murray and MacLeod's reading professionals, bed was the usual place for recreational reading (1995:10), while the *Books Alive* (2001) survey found that the preferred reading locations were 'in bed' and 'on holiday': two cultural locations where normal routines and obligations may be easily ignored.

For the readers, the bedroom is certainly a significant cultural space. Bedroom readers have a high degree of control over their own reading practice as a consequence. Ivana explained that she did most of her reading:

in the bedroom because the house just doesn't have the facilities to have like a place where you can sit, it's a small place, a bedroom and a kitchen and a lounge room where the computer is and the telephone, and things like that which I think is distracting, I always read on the bed basically (I).

The bedroom seems the only space within her small apartment that allows her to avoid distractions. Reading alone in the privacy of the bedroom obviates the need to negotiate the use of space. Similarly, Frances, who really does need silence to get the most from a book, reads mostly 'in bed, when I go to bed, so usually between probably ten, ten-thirty and midnight would be my primary reading time' (F), a 'primary reading time' that is indivisible from the reading space. Other readers also said that bedtime reading was central to their practice:

And why do you choose to read in bed?
Because it's comfortable, and I guess it's a kind of a zone where I'm away from everything else (E).

It's easier just reading, if you're tired you just turn off the light, it's right there (Y).

The bedroom provides a 'zone', a place away from the distractions of others that offers a unique sense of privacy (Manguel 1996:153). This privacy produces a sense of freedom in readers, freedom from the crowding, confinement and conflict associated with the sharing of social spaces (Tuan 1977:64).

Autonomy and solitude are appealing aspects of bedtime reading, but the readers also spoke of another attraction: comfort. The comfort of reading in bed is manifest in two ways. First, book-reading in this context seems to have, like other cultural practices, a ritualistic and participatory function that exists beyond the meaning of the text (Couldry 2000:9). The ritual of reading in bed provides a sense of reassurance and well-being. Terri told me that 'I like to read last thing at night, I can't really sleep unless I read for a while [...] I sort of look forward to it' (T). To this end she selects books for bedtime reading that will prepare her for sleep, books that are good for 'stroking down your mind at the end of the day' (T). Reading is a ritual integral to bedtime: 'it's such a ritual now that it, if I don't [read in bed] I feel really strange, I've got to be really exhausted from a night out and it must be four in the morning before I can sleep without a book' (L). The importance of this bedtime reading ritual to this reader is confirmed by her response to a potential threat to its continuation:

One of the big problems in my life at the moment, which I think I've just resolved by being a bully is to, like, when [my partner] and I are going to sleep at night, I don't turn the light off, I used to get into bed and turn the light off and lie there for three hours thinking, I'd like to be reading a book right now but I can't wake him up. So now when we go to bed, he goes to sleep with the light on and I read my book for a couple of hours, but that, for a few months, was a real pain because I couldn't follow the routine I've been in since I was about four (L).

The anxiety and relief felt by this reader is a marker of the importance of this particular reading ritual. There is also an indication that although bedtime reading may avoid many restrictions, it remains for some a shared space and, therefore, is still capable of producing tension.

Ritualised media consumption of this type provides a structure within which everyday life is naturalised and stabilised (Hermes 1995:24). The use of reading to structure a reader's day is related by Frances who reads magazines in the early evening 'between five and eight' while her mother and father are playing *Scrabble*, after which she'll watch television before going to bed: 'I know that sounds a bit boring but [laughs] watching someone play *Scrabble* but I suppose while I'm watching them I read the newspaper or reading a magazine' (F). Reading magazines requires less attention on her part which allows Frances to be more social, but reading books is reserved for the silence of bedtime. In fact, it is possible to see how Frances structures her evenings through the use of particular media: early evening devoted to magazines, newspapers, some television or handicrafts, often all three simultaneously; middle evening for television, mainly films and drama, and late evening when she reads in bed.

Reading rituals provide a sense of psychological security and comfort. But for some of the readers I interviewed, reading also affords comfort at the level of the physical.

Where do you do most of your reading?
In bed usually.

In bed, is that in the evenings or during the day, do you go to bed and read?
Yes, either, it doesn't matter I don't worry about, I just feel comfortable lying down at peace you know.
Is that why you read it bed?
Yes.
Comfort?
Yes, I just feel comfortable reading in my own room you know (A).

Anthony's bedroom reading is still motivated by a need to avoid distractions, he cannot read on public transport for that reason, but he also emphasises his desire to feel at ease physically. This physical aspect of reading is echoed by Dirk who, despite being able to read anywhere, told me that reading in bed was an ideal:

Occasionally, reading lying down is like you know very relaxing of course if I want to, if I want to do that sort of thing then I will, I mean and I'll only read at the dining table if I'm eating or something like that.

[...]

you know yeah lying, reading in bed it's, it's for relaxation, if you're reading for pleasure then I think it's pretty much the ideal place to do it (D).

This perception of reading in bed as an ideal is also articulated by a female reader, albeit in a different form. For Julie, reading alone and in silence is metaphorically 'like going to bed with a box of chocolates, you know' (J). Reading in her ideal environment gives her a feeling comparable to that of reading in bed, the mention of 'the box of chocolates' reinforces the sensuous, physical pleasure that reading gives her. A link between the body and books is made frequently in the way the readers speak of their reading: reading is 'gorgeous'; to buy books is to go on a 'binge'; readers become 'immersed' in and 'savour' the narrative; 'poor' quality books are 'crappy' or 'shitty'. Metaphors of reading often take their inspiration from the body or bodily functions: 'we, the readers, speak of savouring a book, of finding nourishment in it, of devouring a book at one sitting, of regurgitating or spewing up a text, of ruminating on a passage' (Manguel 1996:170).

Even though bedroom reading was represented as a common ideal, it was not universal. Winston saw reading in bed as a place, not of maximum reading pleasure, but of grudging last resort:

Do you read in bed at all?
Occasionally, yes I can, occasionally but I try to not to because I mean I tend to doze off, the reading position is something that you know, finding a good reading position is hard, lying down, I actually will read lying on the floor, I find this good because ...
Face down?
Both down and up, and then your arms get tired, but that yes something I'm always aware of, it's hard to sort of find a good position, so sometimes you resort to the bed out of desperation (W).

This seems to be a good example of the reading requirements of the body overriding the cognitive engagement with texts: the reading body demands to be placed in a certain position and without an adequate reading position reading is inhibited. Although 'the body' has featured, increasingly, in recent cultural scholarship (Shilling 1993; Coupland and Gwyn 2003), the embodied pleasure of reading is not sufficiently stressed perhaps 'because what is supposedly cerebral turns out to be sensual, even erotic ...' (Game and Metcalfe 1998:139). Yet, as I mentioned earlier, bodily comportment has been, historically, a significant component of past orders of reading.

Despite the marginalisation of reading as an embodied act, my readers stressed the importance of the physical comfort afforded by books. In this general comment from Lana, the appeal of reading goes demonstrably beyond the cognitive:

> I guess there is something magical about reading someone else's words and at
> the same time there's something quite comfortable, comforting about it [...] it's
> always been a good way of being comfortable (L).

Here the conventional mind/body dualism is dissolved as the reader refuses
to privilege one over the other, preferring to equate the imaginative appeal
of reading 'someone else's words' with the bodily 'comfort' that reading
gives her. Zoe made a similar observation: 'reading makes me feel safe, it is
nice and familiar' (Z). The significance that the readers attach to the role of
their bodies in the reading process seems to support the suggestion that
'often the pleasure derived from reading largely depends on the bodily comfort of the reader' (Manguel 1996:151). The most animated example of
bodily reading among the readers was reported by Zoe. Although, like others, she read in bed 'Because it's comfy [laughs]', she also suggested that
'you can sweep from side to side with the page turning [laughs]' (Z). In this
description, which seemed a little embarrassing to relate in an academic
interview, Zoe's bedtime reading practice resembles a dance; the cognitive
and the somatic are fused. Significantly, these meanings and pleasures of the
reading body are invisible to a purely text-based analytical approach.

Spaces of reading: public transport

There are many differences between reading in the home and reading on
the bus or the train; between reading in the comfort and privacy of one's
lounge or bedroom and the uncomfortable, impersonal environment of public transport. Yet, bedrooms and buses do have something in common; they
are both liminal and largely illegitimate cultural spaces. Like bedtime reading, commuter reading is a good example of the spatio-temporal reading
economy, the limits it imposes on reading practice, and the manner in which
these limits are exploited to full effect by everyday readers.

   The invention of public transport was, incidentally, the invention of a new
reading protocol. The advent of railway travel to Britain in the middle of the
nineteenth-century produced a huge increase in reading (Altick 1963:88-89).
The enforced leisure of a rail trip created a new space for reading, while
increasing numbers of railway stations provided a large network for the distribution of print (Williams 1965:73; Schivelbusch 1986:64). The confluence
of reading and commuting is made evident by this American visitor to late
Victorian Britain:

> Sandwiches, oranges, and penny novelettes are the three great requisites for
> English travelling—for third-class travelling at least; and, of the three, the nov-
> elette is by far the most imperative, a pleasant proof of how intellectual needs

outstrip our bodily requirements. The clerks and artisans, shopgirls, dress-makers, and milliners, who pour into London every morning by the early trains, have, each and every one, a choice specimen of penny fiction to beguile the short journey to work, and perhaps the few spare minutes of a busy day (Repplier 1891: electronic source).

As with all such extensions of public access to cultural products 'railway fiction' was ridiculed by cultural critics. Rather than highlighting the significant contribution railway reading and publishing played in the proliferation of reading (Altick 1963:89; Williams 1965:73; Fischer 2003:292), Victorian cultural commentators derided railway fiction and its readers (Williams 1965:190). Half a century later, Q.D. Leavis remained convinced that railway reading was a 'kind of reading that needed little exertion ...' (Leavis 1932:162-63). More books and more readers are always equated with poor books and poor readers—there is a small or in fact non-existent gap between the criticism of a text, or genre, and a value judgement upon the readers of those texts. Thirty years after Q.D. Leavis's study, similarly negative observations were still being made: modern print culture was 'used at the uncritical low attentive level as a kind of drug to kill the dull hours of public transportation or sitting at home with nothing better to do' (De Grazia 1962:327). This carping tradition is continued by those who would agree with George Steiner that 'most modern novels' are 'momentary surface intrusions to be left in the airport lounge' (Steiner 1973:29): illegitimate books read in illegitimate spaces and, I dare say, read by illegitimate readers.

Although Agnes Repplier describes a moment in the cultural lives of late Victorian Londoners, the similarity between late nineteenth-century commuter culture and contemporary commuting is clear: people continue to steal reading time from the impersonal, rationalised routines of the working day. Indeed, among the readers I interviewed, those who relied on public transport indicated that reading on buses and trains comprised a significant portion of their reading time. For instance, the majority of the time Belinda spends reading is time spent in transit to and from her work:

> When I'm on a roll most of it is done when I'm walking to work and back from work or sitting on a bus
> *You read walking along?*
> [laughs] I walk when I read, I've got a lot of rainy stained books [laughs]
> *Do you read on public transport?*
> Yes always (B).

Similarly, Natasha is a commuter reader:

> *Where do you do most of that reading?*
> If I'm reading a book that I'm reading and I'll take it with me and read it on public transport, I'll read it [...] especially on buses, I can't read in a car, if I tried

I'd be puking out the windows but on buses are fine, trains are fine, so I probably do a lot of reading in transit (N).

The amount of reading time that commuting can provide is not lost on Dirk either. When asked if he read on public transport he replied: 'I don't use public transport any more, but when I did yes very much so coz I had probably an hour's journey each way, everyday, there's you know, you can get a fair amount of reading done in that kind of time' (D).

The ubiquitous nature of commuter reading would probably not come as a surprise to anybody who uses public transport. However, the cultural significance of the reading undertaken in such an environment might not be so widely recognised. The opportunity that commuting offers readers seems to contradict de Certeau's (1984) claim that mass transit is a form of 'travelling incarceration' as commuters are 'organized by the gridwork of technocratic discipline, a mute rationalization of laissez-faire individualism' (de Certeau 1984:114). Although it is hard to disagree that travelling to and from work is not part of an impersonal daily routine, I would argue that to regard the space of commuting as culturally and creatively barren is to overlook the importance of the 'enforced leisure' that public transport has offered.

In the light of my conversations with readers, it is difficult to agree that commuters occupy a space in which there is nothing to do and, by implication, nothing is done. The centrality of commuter reading to everyday reading practice is explained here, in some detail, by Georgina:

Where do you do most of your reading?
At the moment it would probably be, on the bus because you know I spend an hour going to work on a bus and you know and I probably [spend] about 10, 12 hours a week on a bus so that's where I get most of my reading done, otherwise if I've got a really long afternoon off I'd, you know, go to the park and grab a cup of coffee which doesn't seem to happen enough. Yeah actually [public] transport is probably where I read the most, it's time where actually you can sit down and not be distracted, and not feeling I should be you know vacuuming or making a phone call to someone or something (G).

Although she reads at home, 'maybe late at night if I can't sleep or if there's reading I've gotta get done [for uni]' Georgina finds it difficult: 'no I kinda find, maybe it's just the house I'm in at the moment, [that] I'm too open to distraction at home' (G). According to this reader, the isolation of public transport affords her a space that she can fill productively. Despite not being her ideal place to read, Georgina nonetheless suggested that she is freer to read on public transport than she is at home. This phenomenon also appears in Catarina's reading. Not only does her reading increase when she's travelling, but her reading actually improves: 'I seem to read better, for some reason, I seem to read better in cars too' (C).

In fact, for some of the readers I interviewed, a reduction in time spent on public transport actually results in a *loss* of reading time. Winston told me that, while he could not read novels on his bus journey to university he did read the newspaper: 'I read the newspaper, which I do for pleasure on the bus, and that's a recent thing, if I'm not on the bus I probably won't read the newspaper' (W). Public transport provides a reading opportunity that otherwise would not exist. For Eric, living closer to university has reduced his daily travelling time by more than two hours. Living nearer to a place of employment or study is usually considered desirable, but Eric does not consider his relocation, from an outer metropolitan to an inner city suburb, to be all positive: 'it takes a good couple of hours out the day when I don't think that I have time to read' (E). Significantly, a reduction in commuting time by an hour has not facilitated an extra hour's reading at home. Another reader also told me that a reduction in commuting time had robbed her of reading opportunities. Lana once needed to take both a bus and a train to get to university and later, while working as a school teacher, she had to endure a long train journey: 'I would read for the forty minutes and I would sit there and read anything I could get my hands on, coz you can't do your marking on the train, it flies everywhere' (L). However, now back in full-time study she has moved into the same suburb as her university and consequently her reading time has been reduced: 'I read a lot less now I live closer to uni' (L). For both Eric and Lana, reading is spatially as well as temporally dependent; the cost of the convenience of living closer to university has been a reduction in their overall leisure reading time.

The opportunity for reading that public transport offers cannot always be taken by readers. The invitation to read that commuting offers has a physical limitation placed upon it. Although much cultural studies analysis tends to ignore any biological influences on cultural activities, one physical limit to commuter reading is impossible to ignore: motion sickness.

> No I can read anytime, but I can't read anywhere, I can't read on public transport for example, I can't do that, I think I get a bit of motion sickness so, so it, it jumps and so I, that's bit of a drawback because I have a lot of time travelling back and forth ... (J).

> *Do you read on public transport?*
> No I can't I get travel sick. I'm very envious of [partner], he can do that (K).

> *Can you read on public transport?*
> No, I get motion sickness and that sucks because it's such a waste of time (Z).

The readers who are affected by motion sickness all realise the lost opportunity that their affliction precipitates.

Reading on public transport can also be undertaken as means of self-defence: reading affords a degree of 'mobile-privatisation' (Williams 1974:26). If reading 'publicises' private spaces, then it may also privatise public spaces. Reading in the home and while travelling on public transport could then be interpreted as an example of a strong counter-current within modernity societies: the simultaneous increase in both the self-sufficiency of the family home and personal mobility (ibid.).[7] People's lives have become simultaneously more public *and* more private: one of the paradoxes of modernity (Giddens 1990:7: Jensen 1990:63). Reading in these instances is perhaps not just about escapism. Far from running blindly away from a dull life, readers are imaginatively *re-connecting* to their location through their reading. In order to manage the increasingly public and impersonal nature of everyday experiences, books are used to create an imaginary distance between one traveller and another, to 'mark a space' (Wise 2000:297), and thus individualise a general social experience. To this end, Lana told me that reading on public transport afforded a sense of comfort on a journey that is often uncomfortable:

> yes, coz generally ... I'm away from the fat guy on the bus who sat on me the other day.
>
> [...]
>
> *So almost [reading] as a form of protection?*
> Oh, very much so. That's my theory about most people who have Walkmans or Discmans is that they can put something in their ears and they lose all that stimulus, so they lose the stimulus of the man next to them, they lose the stimulus of the stink of the vomit left over from Saturday, the bus lurching and all the rest of it (L).

Comfort in this sense differs from the comfort that readers experience when reading in bed. Reading a book on a crowded city bus is, according to Lana, like listening to a personal stereo: it allows for the 'negation of the external environment' (Bull 2000:74); it changes a reader's experience space. The comfort derived from reading on public transport, as an act of self-individuation, is perhaps more psychological than physical. Although, as with Frances's use of reading to make her exercise regime more palatable, it may not be productive to return to a mind/body dualism by separating bodily from psychological phenomena. It is possible to speculate, however, that in both instances reading offers the reader a sense of control over their immediate environment, an example of the way in which '[t]he body is in the text of everyday life; by enacting that text, it becomes not a product but the processor of everyday life' (Cranney-Francis 1995:112).

Conclusion

The readers I interviewed are certainly not 'chaotic readers', neither are they disinterested. They take their reading seriously; novel reading in everyday settings requires a great deal of effort since everyday reading is reading under pressure. Access to reading materials is certainly a limit on all kinds of cultural practices, but in the case of my readers physical access to books is not a barrier. Rather, it is the availability of time and space in which to read that imposes restrictions on reading practices; readers are rarely 'free' to just *read*. Readers are embroiled in an economy of reading in which time and space are scarce commodities and, unlike professional readers, they have to negotiate, purchase or steal, the time and space in which to read; they are 'time bandits' rather than 'semiotic guerillas' (de Certeau 1984). So, while reading in bed and on buses may appear very different they are, in fact, linked. These two reading practices create cultural places through the re-appropriations of time and space. Unlike readers who operate within professional reading economies, everyday readers have to *make* the time to read, time that is 'always-already' allocated by the routines of everyday life, routines that are largely beyond the control of cultural actors. By creating such 'reading places', readers actually construct their everyday cultural worlds because reading transforms their experiences of particular social spaces. In the domain of the home and in the crush of public transport, reading marks the space as what Wise calls 'a place of comfort' (Wise 2000:297). The everyday value of reading in this instance is not to be found in the text, or in the aesthetic, but in the way reading allows readers in a given location to transform it, albeit temporarily, into a 'place' partly of their own making.

Notes

1. Alberto Manguel quotes from *Life of Saint Gregory* in which a twelfth-century monk describes the latrine as a 'retiring place where tablets can be read without interruption' (Manguel 1996:152).
2. Jeanette Gilfedder describes this practice mode as 'interstitial reading' (cited in Lyons 2001:375).
3. Buckridge *et al.* (1995) ask 'the simple triad of questions ... *what*, *why* and *how* do these people read?' (Buckridge *et al.* 1995:23, authors' emphasis), but never ask *where*. The same can be said of Bennett *et al.*'s *Accounting for Taste: Australian Everyday Cultures* (1999).
4. Taksa and Lyons (1992) highlight the degree to which reading 'was condemned as an idle pursuit, which offended against a rather demanding work ethic', one that predominated in working-class families between the wars (Taksa and Lyons 1992:41).

5. This binary relationship between reading books and watching television is found in other studies; for instance, Gemma Moss's (1993) investigation of romance reading among teenage girls. Moss found that while her teenage readers could read as much as they wished, too much time spent in front of the television elicited a parental rebuke (Moss 1993:124).

6. Eagleton (1983) makes the point that some nineteenth-century conservatives saw silent reading as a technique for social control: 'since reading is an essentially solitary, contemplative activity,' it would, 'curb in them [the lower-classes] any disruptive tendency to collective political action' (Eagleton 1983:25).

7. Nigel Thrift (1996) suggests that social interaction occurs over increasingly large distances: '[f]actors such as commuting and the increased mobility associated with white-collar jobs have assured this is so' (Thrift 1996:83).

3 'You Give a Bit of Yourself When You Give a Book': Books, Readers and Social Networks

What we call consumption rituals are the normal modes of friendship.
Mary Douglas and Baron Isherwood, *The World of Goods*

... everything bears witness to what we are, our friendships, our enmities, our glance and the clasp of our hand, our memory ...
Frederich Nietzche, *Untimely Mediations*

Introduction

The readers I surveyed all speak of the limits which time and space impose upon their everyday reading. The availability or otherwise of a place in which to read is a constitutive element of their practice. The time and space of reading are then part of the enabling infrastructure that is masked by those models of reading which concentrate solely upon the relationship between the singular reader and the text. If the spatio-temporal economy of everyday reading is often hidden from view, then so is the social. The term social economy refers to the networks of local relationships within which everyday reading is practised. In this chapter, I examine the operation of these informal socio-cultural networks or 'proto-communities' that are constituted through shared cultural consumption (Willis 1990). Such proto-communities provide valuable reading resources and, as social 'intermediaries' (Thrift 1996), books become a means by which readers maintain social relationships within an environment where friendship is increasingly the product of self-reflexive negotiation. Within the readers' everyday print culture, books may be used to increase their sociality; the exchange of books is a way of *doing* friendship. Book exchanges, in material and symbolic forms, provide readers with both an index of intimacy and with materials that may be deployed in creative acts of self-representation. The functional and expressive role of books within an everyday social economy of reading is a further aspect of book culture that cannot be read *off the text*.

From the solitary to the social reader

In his modestly titled general text, *How to Read and Why* (2001), Harold Bloom goes to some lengths to stress the singularity of readers and reading. 'We read,' he asserts, 'not only because we cannot know enough people, but because friendship is so vulnerable, so likely to diminish or disappear, overcome by space, time, imperfect sympathies, and all the sorrows of familial and passional life' (Bloom 2001:2). In the same sentence as he draws an analogy between books and friends, that is, that they both expose the reader to 'otherness', Bloom also claims that reading actually constitutes a retreat of the self from the social. The perception that reading is an individual act is stated clearly in the didactic UNESCO publication *Roads to Reading* (1979). 'Reading', the author asserts without fear of contradiction, 'is usually considered a solitary act', an act that is constituted through 'interaction between the ideas of the writer and the brain of the reader' (Staiger 1979:22). For both Bloom and UNESCO's anonymous scribe, reading is, first and foremost, something that occurs within the mind of the individual reader.

Through this 'ideology of the solitary reader' (Long 1993; 2003), the 'foundational infrastructure' that enables reading as a cultural practice is obscured. As Elizabeth Long has argued, 'reading must be taught and that socialization into reading always takes place within specific social relationships' (Long 1993:191). These social or economies of reading are most obvious when books are consumed within formal educational environments or in the context of semi-formal organisations, as is the case with fan-clubs or reading groups. In addition to these discrete cultural formations, reading also occurs within other, less formal, and less public social groupings (Korhonen 2006: electronic source). These more informal networks are a feature of Radway's *Reading the Romance* (1984) which examines, at some length, the manner in which romance reading is implicated in the domestic and social relationships of the Smithton women. Despite such concerns, however, Radway does not focus at any great length on the role that books and reading may have within more widely constituted friendship networks.

The correlation between friendship and reading that my research uncovered may have been a product of the research method itself because the manner in which potential subjects are recruited will have a considerable influence on the findings of the research (Geraghty 1998:145). As I explained in Chapter One, a significant number of the readers who collaborated in this research were found through pre-existing social networks where 'one starts with a member of the desired group and then asks for recommendations of friends, neighbours and relatives to be included' (Geraghty 1998:146). By using a number of pre-existing social networks to locate potential interviewees it is logical to expect that there will be a connection between friendship and reading: readers are unlikely to recommend that the interviewer contact a non-reading friend. The willingness and confidence with which readers were prepared to 'volunteer' their reading friends is an indication perhaps of the significance of reading within that relationship. This methodological choice may be responsible for a major difference between my research and that of Buckridge *et al* who found that 'reading lacked a social or even familial dimension' (Buckridge *et al* 1995:26). This having been said it is important to note that the social nature of reading within my study is not simply a by-product of methodology. Despite the influence of the method of selection, other readers who had not been located through 'snowballing' also indicated that reading and exchanging books were practices that they shared with friends.

This chapter examines this social economy of everyday reading, but, before discussing the part played by books within voluntary social networks, it would be remiss not to at least outline the first social relationship within which readers find themselves: reading within the family.

'All in the family': growing-up reading

The readers all grew up in an environment that actively encouraged and valued reading, not just novels, but a wide range of printed texts. While not all readers necessarily enjoyed reading at school or at university, none told me that they had any difficulties acquiring their reading skills. All the readers reported that they had read from a young age:

When did you first start reading?
I really don't know, quite young I used to, I used to have a say in what books I read, my mother would encourage me so maybe about seven, eight I'd really be directing what I read and then by twelve I would be pretty keen to read particular books (B).

Goodness ... well when do you go to school? Just before going to school, three and a half, four (J).

Well I won't be able to remember but I know from what my mum and day say about it I've always read lots. I was one of those children that they ... kept taking for hearing tests because they, I wouldn't answer when they talked to me because I was reading a book yeah (K).

I think, I was very young, maybe younger than I remember (I).

I can't remember ... not reading, I remember learning to read very clearly and making the words ... my parents were away a lot when I was a child and my grandmother used to read to me all the time ... (T).

Did your parents read a lot?
One parent did, my Mum reads a lot my Dad doesn't, he reads the newspaper, he doesn't read books very often probably one a year (F).

And what type of books does your Mum read?
Well now, well most of my life she has read whatever book I got from the library so that [laughs] she read teenage books when I was reading teenage books, and now we read mostly the same but, pretty much we read a pretty big range of everything no specific sort of style or anything (F).

What are some of your earliest reading memories?
Probably ... the *Narnia Chronicles* by C.S. Lewis ... they were read to me as a very young child and then of course I re-read them, and re-read them, and re-read them, after a while I then moved on to other stuff later on (D).

Would you describe your house as a reading house?
Oh yeah! very much so yeah I've always, my mother was already encouraging me to read, and I've always read (D).

The influence of parents was a predominant feature of all the readers' reading histories, across the entire age-range (21 to 51 years of age). Not surprisingly, parental attitudes are a major influence on children's leisure reading (Greaney and Hegarty 1987:3). Less predictably this influence also seems to have come from parents who were not themselves avid readers: 'they certainly encouraged me to read, [...] but they didn't love literature, they certainly never guided my reading beyond childhood, [but] reading was a, a good thing (W); 'they didn't read at all ... but they did respect it [reading] if that makes any sense?'(T). Among the readers' parents the conventional gender division was also heavily represented: fiction-reading mothers appear more frequently than fathers. One reader told me that although her mum and dad are both readers, her dad 'wouldn't admit to it, but he is I reckon' (C). When reading fathers are mentioned it is most often in connection with non-fiction reading: newspapers, magazines, biographies and 'history books'.

In an effort perhaps to maximise their historical relationship with 'the book', some readers told me that they could read 'before they could read', by which they meant that they were *read to* by a parent, elder sibling or carer, before they themselves acquired the requisite skills:

Reading myself, I was reading by the time I was four. So, by the time I went to school, I guess I was ... you know reading children's books. But I think I thought of myself as reading when my mother and father used to read me stories, so that was from a very young, even younger, probably two or three ... but taking library books, ... and initiating my own reading probably six or seven (J).

Despite the strong parental influence—'I think my father's one sort of aim was to make me a reader' (L)—others recounted their reading histories in a way which emphasised the relationship between reading books and cultural autonomy:

> My father used to read to me when I was a kid and that was sort of a big marker of when I started to grow-up and I didn't want him to read to me any more and that was, like, a sad thing for both of us (W).

> *Were your mum and dad big readers?*
> No, my mother is but, she, her taste didn't have a particular impact on my own (B).

The theme of autonomy is continued by Roz who provides more details of the relationship between her parents' reading and her own:

> mum used to read Jackie Collins and that kind of crap stuff, dad would read technical manuals and science things so they didn't really influence my reading.
> *They didn't?*
> No, apart from mum buying me *Clan of the Cave Bear* or and, what was the other one I read? Science fiction, I read science fiction too.

> *So if your mum and dad didn't influence your reading, who did?*
> ... me I think [laughs] I don't know anyone who did. We used to go to the library once a week and I used to come out with 17 books or so, in one go (R).

In this interview extract, Roz appears to have a very narrow definition of 'influence', a definition limited to the types or genres of books read. In fact, she seems almost to be erasing the social economy of reading from her own early reading history. Being bought books and being taken to the library do not seem to count as an 'influence', even though her mother's actions would have facilitated reading in an important material sense. The correlation between self-initiated reading and cultural autonomy is continued by another reader who drew special attention to the moment when she could read by herself:

> *At what age did you first begin reading for pleasure?*
> Very early, before I started school, not sure of the age, I can't remember being read to, my mother tells me that she read me stories but when I learned to read myself, I didn't want to be read to (K).

Reading to 'one's self' becomes a marker of independence, a stage in the journey toward adulthood: to be symbolically in charge of books, of narrative, is to perhaps be a 'self'.

Friendship and modernity

After growing up in environments where reading was part of the *habitus*, it is not surprising that books have continued to be a feature of the readers' cultural worlds. Within their everyday cultural domain, books are valued as a medium for the initiation and maintenance of friendships; the giving, lending and recommending of books, as a mode of exchange, operate to both support and constitute the interplay of social actors.

The contemporary notion of friendship, that of intimate friendship, is a modern phenomenon closely associated with the rise of individualism (Oliker 1998:18). Accompanying this development of individualism—an identity not simply determined by 'lineage, gender, social status'—is an ironic understanding that the modern self is increasingly a 'reflexive' project in which the individual strives to sustain 'coherent, yet continuously revised, biographical narratives, ... in the context of multiple choice as filtered through abstract systems' (Giddens 1991:5). Friendships are a part of this 'reflexive project' in that they contribute to the production of self-identity. Crucial to the creation and continuation of friendships are exchange and interaction (Willmot 1987), and these interactions between social actors are often 'supported by relational symbols, rituals, and ceremonies' (O'Connor 1992:50 and 147). Further, Nigel Thrift suggests that 'intermediaries'—texts, artefacts, people, money—actually constitute rather than just support interaction: 'intermediaries ... allow networks to come into being by giving social links shape and consistency' (Thrift 1996:24). The exchange of books and book-talk are examples of social 'intermediaries': '*things* that draw actors into relationships' (ibid., original emphasis).

Friendships are then built through interactions, but the possibility for such interaction is always bounded because people always have limited 'funds of sociability' (Allen 1979:117). In conventional usage, sociability refers to a person's inclination to spend time in the company of others. However, as a consequence of the social patterns of modernity, there is always a limit to the time that social actors may spend in direct social proximity. Paradoxically, while it reduces physical contact, modernity also introduces new conduits for relationships: friendships may be initiated and sustained at a distance (Giddens 1990; Thompson 1995; Thrift 1996; Allen 1998). This defining feature of modernity has been made possible by the development of technologies such as print, the telegraph, telephone and digital telecommunications that have all facilitated increased contact between people who are geographically dispersed and temporally displaced. These cultural technologies extend a cultural actor's 'funds of sociability' by facilitating a mode of interaction that operates beyond periods of face-to-face contact.

The exchange of books between friends is most likely to be regarded as a form of symbolic exchange that operates beyond the parameters of a capitalist economy. The value of such informal 'gifts' is measured solely within the social relationship in which it is given (Slater 1997:53). Consequently, the social relationships themselves would normally be placed outside the orbit of commerce (Frow 1997:145). Distinctions of this nature help maintain the barrier between the public realm of commodities and the private domain of gifts. It may be possible to argue however that, when used as a way of increasing a person's 'funds of sociability', the giving of books as gifts may circulate in a different sort of economy; an economy not driven by social obligation, as in the 'gift economy', nor profit as in the capitalist, but by a desire to establish, maintain and manage relationships.

Seen in this light, books have both instrumental and expressive use-values. Instrumental use-value is the property of a cultural text or object that allows a goal to be reached or a task to be undertaken (Willis 2001:19). For example, as I outlined in the previous chapter, books have an instrumental use-value in that they may ameliorate a reader's unpleasant experiences of commuting. In comparison, expressive use-value is an object or text's capacity to signify something to both the self and to others: 'signification is never far away as precondition, medium, outcome' (Willis 2001:20). This distinction between instrumental and expressive use-values is made in *Reading the Romance*. On the one hand, Radway argues that the instrumental value of romance reading was the creation of a cultural space within the home that was, temporarily, free from the demands of domestic duties. On the other, the expressive value of the Smithton women's reading was one of disconnection: the reading of romances was an indication of the women's discontent within patriarchy. Among the readers I interviewed, books have both instrumental and expressive use-value. Books are used to mark and maintain relationships, and to express something about their constituent cultural actors. Books may operate as 'sign-vehicles' for the performance of particular social identities (Goffman 1959:14).

Proto-communities

The informal social networks in which the readers read constitute what Willis describes as a 'proto-community'. Such proto-communities:

> may sometimes have organic features in that they involve, for instance, direct communication around a 'consuming interest' .... [t]hey may arise in eclectic combinations of consumers who discover, incidentally, that they share a taste or interest as they meet in friendship, neighbourhood, school or workplace groups (Willis 1990:141).

These communities, based on acts of creative consumption, become increasingly significant as employment, geographical and class location become a less secure foundation on which to construct a communal identity. 'One's identity where one lives,' as Marcus argues, 'is only one social context, and perhaps not the most important in which it [identity] is shaped' (Marcus 1992:314).[1] The most ready example of communities based in a 'consuming interest', rather than a particular locale, is organised fandom, but there are other less obvious examples. For example, Sarah Thornton describes the 'taste cultures' of *clubbers* and *ravers* in a way that seems to exemplify a community that, while being far more fluid than certain forms of official fandom, is still based upon shared cultural consumption (Thornton 1995:3). Unlike some representations of everyday culture, which stress its egalitarian nature, Thornton emphasises that taste-cultures, even those thought to mark 'popular' taste, are fundamentally discriminatory. All forms of taste, whether 'high' or 'low', both unite and separate, as they trace the lines of distinction which separate insiders from outsiders (Bourdieu 1984:56).

Proto-communities may take many different forms. Delineated through shared cultural practices and the social relationships which accompany them, these communities are increasingly less the direct product of communal living. Proto-communities, no longer a consequence of a fixed relationship within a stable 'social' realm, are rather the product of 'affectual sharing' (Maffesoli 1996:135). A particular cultural practice can no longer, according to Maffesoli, be simply correlated with a fixed social position; a rigid and knowable social realm has been replaced by a complex web of 'sociality' because, as Willis suggests, '[n]o one knows what the social maps are any more, there are no automatic belongings, so more than ever, you have to work for, and make, your own cultural significance' (Willis 2001:vx). As a result, particular social or class groups cannot be seen to possess wholly distinct and separate cultural practices, and perhaps never could be (Frow 1996:1). A particular social group may then no longer possess a distinct cluster of exclusive cultural practices. The membership of a proto-community may draw on cultural actors from different social or class groups. However, individuals from some social groups may be more active in particular proto-communities than others.

The majority of readers interviewed for this study are women from middle-class socio-economic backgrounds. The central role of women in the operation of reading proto-communities is historically well-documented. Martyn Lyons, looking at mid nineteenth-century European reading practices, writes that books, both fictional and didactic, 'changed hands through exclusively female networks' (Lyons 1998:320). The gender specificity of 'borrowing networks' is also noted in studies of early twentieth-century Australian readership (Taksa and Lyons 1992:124). Similarly, in their study of every day literacy in a northern English town, Barton and Hamilton concluded that the '[leisure activities] people participated in were often gendered' (Barton and Hamilton 1998:171), and that the exchange of books was a gendered activity: women were more likely to share books with female friends than anyone else. The ability of texts to mediate relationships remotely, to extend a reader's 'funds of sociability', may go some way to explain the frequency of book borrowing among female friends who may not be as free to meet in person as frequently as their male counterparts. Reading as a cultural practice has been accessible to women because it is an activity that can be accommodated within the parameters of their conventional social responsibilities: paid work, domestic work and family (Henderson *et al* 1989:108). Certainly within the group of readers I interviewed, who were themselves mostly women, reading friends seemed to be predominantly, although not exclusively, female. In addition, my readers were also overwhelming middle-class in terms of socio-economic background and education. This finding supports Guldberg's study which found that book exchanges were most frequent among middle-class professionals and the tertiary educated (Guldberg 1990:48).

Proto-communities, influenced but not crudely determined by gender and class, operate at the level of the local to create a shared culture analogous to Howard Becker's art or media world (Becker 1982). Below the more organised, regimented and visible interpretative communities, 'affectual sharing' continues at the micro-level where a reader's proto-community may comprise just a few people. Nearly all the readers I interviewed were part of informal proto-communities of book readers while, simultaneously, holding memberships of numerous other 'interpretative' communities (Fish 1980), themselves founded in other cultural forms or practices. I favour the term 'proto-community' over the more common interpretative community, because networks of readers operate in ways that go beyond just the collective interpretation of cultural texts. In the following interview extract, Terri provides a sketch of some aspects of her reading proto-community:

> there's a meeting point there for a relationship really, because it's a really intimate thing sharing a book and I did this recently with a friend of mine, you know Lily Brett? She's just a popular writer, [...] there was this book of essays, I bought it and gave it to my friend, she thought okay essays ... I'll read this, and she sort of seized a lot of the same things I did [...] and, anyway, so she took up weight-lifting because this particular author was talking about the body and that she'd suddenly found her physicality again after a lot of years and four children whatever and ... yeah and now we've got this thing going we're reading various bits of this person's work and it's something that we talk about and that we have together, you know and we have this—this writer has a very intimate voice, so it's like a third friend almost (T).

This is an example of a proto-community in its most immediate form. The striking element in this excerpt is the high degree of intimacy between Terri, her friend, and the books that they share. This intimacy is signalled by the frequent use of the inclusive 'we': 'we've got this thing going'; 'we're reading'; 'something we talk about'; 'we have together'; and 'we have this'. The text provides a common ground, 'a meeting point', a place from which to interact, to talk with each other. This connection between Terri and her friend is further reinforced by the production of shared interpretations: 'she sort of seized on a lot of the same things' (T). Connections are made through shared meanings as well as shared texts. In this fashion, books become a domain in which these two women actually 'do friendship' (Cherland 1994:100). Books and their authors within this proto-community are significant enough to warrant personification: 'it's like having a third friend almost' (T).

Books and friendship networks

Friendships, within the contemporary 'media culture' (Kellner 1995), are mediated and facilitated by cultural commodities. Book choices are, as a consequence, implicated in readers' social identities. Karen Harrison, in her discussion of middle-class women's friendships, argues that 'identity is marked out through the use of symbols. There is an association between the things a person uses, the things a person does, and the image presented by their personal and collective identities' (Harrison 1998:102). The success or otherwise of a book exchange has, therefore, implications for a particular construction of self; a construction that relies upon shared recognition for its efficacy. The use-value of a particular book-exchange may then be its ability to articulate a particular representation of self, as '[c]ultural practices of meaning-making are intrinsically self-motivated as aspects of identity-making and self-construction: in making our cultural world we make ourselves' (Willis 2001:xiv).

Friends and books: what the readers say

Among the people I interviewed, friends are the biggest single source of knowledge of reading materials. This phenomenon is evident in Natasha's proto-community where friends and relatives are her main source of books:

> going into a bookshop and looking at books is not something I would normally do, usually I kinda borrow them off friends, my dad's got a huge collection of books and a lot of the books I read I've found on his bookshelf... (N).

This reader, like Natasha, has many friends who read:

> I'm surrounded by people who love to read and who've got more time than me. [...] I have a lot of friends who are retired and they normally give me books, so for example I received three books on my birthday and about five at Christmas time (J).

For Georgina, Karen and Terri, recommendations from friends guide their reading:

> I suppose its recommendation from people who've read their stuff before and really liked it, that's what I read (G).

> yes, yes, I rely a lot on friends (K).

> friends might suggest that they have read something and really loved it, and that will influence me (T).

According to *Young Australians Reading* (2001), friends first become a reader's 'main source of book advice' during the period spent at high school (*Young Australians Reading* 2001:30). This would suggest that reading proto-communities actually develop in parallel with institutional orders of reading, rather than replacing them after adolescent readers finish school. The significance of reading friends is also made by the *Books Alive* survey which found that, of the people interviewed, 53 per cent gained knowledge of books by 'word of mouth' (*Books Alive* 2001:11 and 40). In contrast to Buckridge *et al*'s 'reading professionals' (1995), only three readers told me that they relied on the literary media for information about books, and only one of those specified a particular medium: *Spectrum*, the arts supplement of the *Sydney Morning Herald*. It is perhaps not a coincidence that this particular reader worked in a large bookshop for a number of years where reading the literary media was a work requirement.

Book exchanges

Friends act as a source of reading material through the exchange of books. Friends may exchange books in different ways. In a material sense, books are lent and given as presents, and so may function as elements in other social rituals. Books may also be 'given' symbolically, in the form of reading recommendations. In the following interview excerpt, Julie explains how she recommends books that she has read and enjoyed:

> the last few books I've recommended, I either lend to my family, they'll just read it because they will read anything or they're friends and I'll only recommend the books I like, yeah that I think they'll like ...
>
> [...]
>
> I try to match the book to the person. But I probably would be annoyed if they didn't read them yeah (J).

Like Julie, Lana often recommends books to others; here she recounts her rationale for giving books as presents and her method of book selection:

> *Why do you give books as presents?*
> Coz I love books. [...] I'm a didactic person [laughs] what do you expect? ... I buy [my partner] books to try and indoctrinate him, try and get him reading and I know that's horrible but, ... I yeah buy books for people ... when I've read them, almost 90 per cent of the time it's because I've read them, unless it's a reference book or something, in fact more than 90 probably 98 per cent and because I liked them and I've thought of conversations I've had with friends that would make them applicable to that friend or instances in their live that they find valuable (L).

Although Lana regards herself as 'didactic' and speaks of indoctrination, this drive to instruct is not unreflective. Rather than foisting any particular book on her reading friends, she takes into account the interests and the 'reading biography' of the intended receiver. Significant too is the fact that '98 per cent' of the books she recommends, or gives, are ones that she herself has liked. The didactic streak in book-lenders is also evident in this comment from Terri:

> If I really think that X would like this [book] and there is something, that ... sometimes there is something I want them to know and or I want to share with them, ... that's a really nice way to do it or you might buy the book for them so you can talk about it ... (T).

In comparison to the confident lending of Lana and Terri, Madelaine will give guidance if she has 'a feel for their taste ... otherwise not' (M). To recommend a book without knowing the reading interests of the recipient is to rely on her own judgement. Without such knowledge: 'I can only say that I myself enjoyed it' (M). For this reader, personal taste alone does not always seem a secure basis upon which to offer a recommendation.

To give or to recommend certain books is the giving of a particular *experience* of reading, an experience that the reader has enjoyed and feels the need to share. The desire to share an experience is articulated by Anthony who speaks here of an attempt to exchange a book with his girlfriend:

> I recommended *Sons and Lovers* to my girlfriend, ... she started reading it and really loved it and ... but she stopped about a quarter of the way through and I've noticed the book there a quarter of the way through over the past two months [laughs] and a couple of times I asked [her] if she was gunna keep reading it, although it's not really my business too, so I stopped ... [...] it was almost like I was pushing her, well in my mind perhaps I wanted her to read it.
> *Why did you want her to read it?*
> I hoped her knowledge would get broadened into reading classic novels if she actually got an interest, possibly interested in writing too, and coming to study at uni and that.

Does she read a lot?
No ... she's, she's got very square eyes ... [laughs] she loves television (A).

The book exchange—the lending of D.H. Lawrence's *Sons and Lovers*—is a textual invitation to his girlfriend to become part of Anthony's reading proto-community. The book exchange is an initial step to align his girlfriend more directly with his cultural domain, even though he represents his motivation as altruistic rather than evangelical. However, his desire that she like 'classic' novels, be interested in writing and university, corresponds with his own cultural interests: Anthony writes fiction for a hobby and attends university part-time. By his own admission the conscious effort to induct his girlfriend into his reading community seems to have been unsuccessful: television, often the readers' nemesis, has carried the day.

A successful book exchange can be seen as a measure of the depth of a friendship, but the failure of the recipient to enjoy, or read, the book can make the giver feel insecure. For example, Ivana told me that although she does not feel offended when friends fail to enjoy a book she has recommended, she does nonetheless feel a degree of 'embarrassment' (I). This feeling of insecurity is elaborated by Susan who explained how significant book exchanges were in her life: 'you hope that people will like the book as much as you do ... if they don't you feel depressed, rejected ... you're passing on something of yourself when you pass on a book' (S). In this case, the need to share an experience of reading is accompanied by a need for personal validation. Susan's sentiments here are akin to those expressed by anthropologist Marcel Mauss. In stressing the importance of social relations embodied in objects, Mauss argues that:

> if one gives things and returns them, it is because one is giving and returning 'respects'—we still say 'courtesies'. Yet it is also because by giving one is giving *oneself*, and if one gives *oneself*, it is because one 'owes' *oneself*—one's person and one's goods—to others (Mauss cited in Dant 1999:8, original emphasis).

If a successful book exchange produces positive feelings, then the opposite also seems to be the case. The effect of an unsuccessful book exchange is narrated here by Natasha:

> if it has been an important book to me, for instance I read *The Skin of A Lion* and lent it to a friend who went overseas recently and she wrote me an email to me saying that it was fantastic and I assumed that she'd finished reading it and then I talked to her about it and she hadn't, and I was kind of worried, you do feel slightly ... miffed [laughs] ... (N).

As Mauss suggests, the recipient of a gift shifts from being in credit, to being indebted, to the gift-giver (Mauss 1967:35). In this case, Natasha's friend has accrued a debt that must be paid through a reading of the given text. The sense of indebtedness that the recipient of a book may feel is expressed by Georgina who, after being given a rather long novel, told me that as 'it was a present from my friend so I'm going to have to read it', even though 'you just wanna get away from it' (G). The giving and reading of books, in this context, becomes part of 'the opening of the individual to the other' that is fundamental to the process of building relationships under the conditions of modernity; conditions where friendships no longer arise 'naturally' from a person's immediate local community (Giddens 1990:121).

No longer a given, relationships have to be negotiated: 'an individual's social identity depends largely on mutual recognition, combined with the self-validation of this recognition' (Kellner cited in Harrison 1998:102). The close association between a book's perceived qualities and the relation between the lender or giver, and the borrower or receiver, is outlined by this reader:

> *What happens if you recommend a book to someone, or you give a book as a present to someone, and that person then doesn't read it?*
> I get really offended [laughs].
> *Why do you get offended?*
> Because they don't like the book and I loved it to death generally.
> *So why should you feel bad if they don't like a book you liked?*
> If they don't like the book I liked then they don't like me! It's a pure reflection thing (R).

According to Roz, the giving of books entails a risk of rejection: if a friend dislikes a recommended book, then that recommendation will reflect badly on herself. This rejection is two-fold: first, the degree to which a friend likes a book is a measure of the present-giver's knowledge of them—knowing what they would like to read is an index of intimacy. This index of intimacy is manifest in Frances's comments regarding her failed book exchanges:

> ah it doesn't really bother me, sometimes I'm surprised only because I tend to recommend a book, like you wouldn't recommend a book that your friend wouldn't like, you'd only recommend the one you thought they'd like any-way so there ... sometimes you think, you know, you think I didn't know that person that's all ... (F).

While Frances does not 'feel like it reflects on me or something like that', it does cause her to question how well she knows her friend. Allied to this misjudgement by a book lender is a second mode of rejection: the failure of a particular representation of self. This desire for intimacy and self-validation may also impact on some of the readers' attitudes towards 'book' or 'gift' tokens. The token has exchange value within the capitalist economy and may also function to meet the obligation of ritual gift-giving on occasions such as birthdays and Christmas. But the degree to which such tokens contribute to the flow of sociability is less certain. It is possible to interpret the giving of a token as a present, rather than a book, as indicative of the giver being 'out of touch' with the recipient: 'these days I get book vouchers [...] I think it's because most of my family don't know what my taste is. It's been about ... six years since I actually got a book as a present' (L). It is possible to regard this statement as a reluctant acknowledgment that a social or cultural gap has opened between the concerned parties.

Book exchanges—of both the material and symbolic kind—constitute a part of the reciprocity that, Graham Allen argues, is the key issue in the maintenance of friendships outside the family (Allen 1998:77). The absence of book exchanges where they once existed, as a failure in reciprocity, could indicate a change in the status of a relationship:

> When I was at high school my closest friend was a voracious reader, she and I used to pass books on to each other back and forth, for ten years we did that we've now diverged professionally and socially quite a lot so we don't really do that any more, she's got this idea, she calls me her 'intellectual friend', which I think is a big joke and she sort of sees the sort of thing I read as impenetrable and because she's ... training and doing marketing it's not applicable to her she thinks (L).

Lana speaks of her friend's linking of reading with occupational status: to her friend, different occupations call, apparently, for different recreational reading. Where book exchanges were once a marker of affiliation between friends, an affirmation of sameness, their absence symbolises a degree of social and professional separation. If the 'patterned flow of consumption goods' may 'show a map of social integration' (Douglas and Isherwood 1996:xxii), then differences or breaks in that pattern may indicate the opposite.

The importance of consumption as a marker of social integration may, in some cases, extend to even the most intimate of personal relationships. In her interview, Georgina told me that she refused to have romantic or sexual relationships with men who did not read fiction. She narrated a lengthy story of meeting a prospective male partner at a party, staying until the early hours of the morning in order to be alone with him, only to discover that he did not read. When, in the course of discussion he informed her that reading fiction was a 'waste of time' she promptly went home: not reading 'was a big nail in the coffin' (G). The role of cultural commodities in the selection of sexual partners is discussed by Martin Cloonan who shows how, among younger consumers at least, an individual's taste in popular music is thought to affect both one's chances of attracting sexual partners and an individual's view of the opposite sex (Cloonan 1997:2). It is possible to speculate, in light of Georgina's story, that other cultural forms, in this case books, may be used in the same way.

Book exchanges: good and bad

Book exchanges, entangled as they are within networks of social relationships, may then entail a certain amount of personal risk. Such personal or emotional risk may be behind Winston's rule against giving books as gifts: 'I used to have a rule against giving books as presents because I thought, I thought that is was such a, you know, [not giving books] as a guideline because it's such a hard thing to give people books' (W). Despite his reservations, however, as Winston has discovered, such a risk can pay dividends:

> I have a family friend who every Christmas gives me a book and she's reads a lot of stuff and a lot of good stuff contemporary good stuff and invariably gives me something that I wouldn't normally read and I love it so last Christmas it was, and it was fantastic so now I've started ... breaking that rule more often (W).

While the readers spoke of the feelings of rejection that can be experienced when a recommendation is not followed or not liked, they also spoke of the personal satisfaction that comes from a successful book exchange. Catarina, who recommends and lends books both to her friends and her mother, recalled with relish the success of a book exchange that seems to have been long in the planning:

> yes ... it was a big triumph, I was hounding [my friend] for ages and ages and ages to read *1984* ... and he wouldn't do it until I gave him a copy, mine [laughs], and it was a big, big triumph.
> *Why?*
> Because I knew he'd really like it (C).

Clearly, Catarina expresses a sense of pride in her ability to persuade her friend to read a book she *knew* he would like. Her ability to predict her friend's favourable response to *1984* indicates, palpably, the closeness and solidity of their relationship. In an attempt to analyse the significance of book exchanges it is important not to overlook the possibility that there is a simple, but rewarding, pleasure to be gained from contributing to the pleasure of others. Books are an 'emotional currency' since people take time and 'expend a certain amount of emotional energy' when exchanging texts (Cherland 1994:101). In comparison, Catarina's book-exchanges with her mother appear to be driven by other desires:

> That's a big thing if I can get her [mum] to read one of mine.
> *Why is it a big thing?*
> ... just because it's kind of, she's always been the one whose given books to me, it's kind of you know, I'm getting up on her level a little bit, or she's always very polite but we don't like the same things so [laughs] ... (C).

Unlike the lending of Orwell's *1984* to her friend, these exchanges with her mother seem to be motivated by a need for reciprocity, for recognition— something it seems hard for her to attain. The fact that Catarina's mother is a secondary school teacher may add a further layer to the transaction: her mother's recognition may also be partly an institutional legitimation of Catarina's book culture.

Individual readers within their reading communities exchange books for different reasons, take different risks, and experience different rewards. The impact that the relational context has on a book exchange is related by Eric. When I asked him to articulate how he felt when people failed to read or disliked the books he recommended, he said: 'it depends on the person' (E). Unprompted, he elaborated on his response:

> if it is someone I respect like my father who influenced my reading a lot I do get pissed off, because I've read so much of what he's recommended to me that I kind of think that I've invested time in his ... ... in his tastes or, or what he recommends and I've gone off and read myself and kind of recommended back to him and he doesn't, isn't interested, or he'll scan through a book, I use scan, he's not taking it seriously, ... I read *Crime and Punishment* and gave him *Crime and Punishment* and he said it's, it's a melodrama and I immediately got really angry, like I really hate that kind of ... to me if you read that book and you were willing to brush it off with one word you haven't really read it properly and I kind of see that as personally insulting (E).

In exchanging books with his father, Eric seems to want reciprocity from a reader who is very much part of his reading community. There could be also some 'canonical weight' behind Eric's complaint. Not only has his father dismissed a text that Eric values, but he has described a book that is often positioned as a 'classic' novel as a 'melodrama', a term that is most often used pejoratively. This very intense response to a failed book exchange with an 'insider' is then compared with a hypothetical transaction between Eric and an 'outsider':

> I think, I think I'd be more impressed had I learnt that they did read it ... so it would be kind of converse, that if I recommended something and they had gone out and found it, it would be like a compliment [...] and they've actually broached the subject with me again, yeah, it's kinda like a pat of the back I guess (E).

When exchanging books with readers with whom he is less well-acquainted, Eric's feelings are palpably different. A 'return' on the recommendation, on the 'gift', is not expected in this instance, therefore, a failure to reciprocate has less social significance.

Marking a self

Books are exchanged both materially, books are lent or given as gifts, and symbolically in the form of recommendations. As well as speaking of the degree of social vulnerability integral to these exchanges, my readers also spoke of exposure to a financial or material risk. Some readers related a fear that once lent, a book would not be returned:

> *Do you lend books?*
> I've had bad experiences with lending books to people and not getting them back I mean I've got a friend who has about five or six of my books [...] I try not to any more lend books to people I just buy them [one] for their birthday unless it's someone I really know, if you know what I mean [laughs] ... (G).

> Yeah, yeah I often lend books out yeah and get very annoyed when they don't come back of course (K).

> I do, I do but I, I'm not a very good lender, it's the same with my music because I've been screwed over a few times so ... I'd love to be Mr Freelove and hand everything around but there is reasons why I don't I suppose (E).

In contrast there was a distinct minority, represented here by Natasha, who seemed to care little for books as material objects:

> I lend books to friends with awareness that they may never come back [laughs] but I kind of think it is a silly thing to keep books simply because ... you know I'm planning to go overseas next year and I don't know how many years I'll be way for so, to keep books, because I don't read books twice, I kind of not really attached to them (N).

With few exceptions, most readers expressed a fear of losing a commodity which they had purchased but considering that books, especially when bought second-hand, are sometimes cheaper that magazines, it is unlikely the fear of losing a book is solely or even predominantly financial.

For some readers, having a book close at hand makes re-reading convenient. Re-reading is a frequent activity among a high proportion of the readers. Over half the readers reported that they re-read books, in order to return to favourite a text, or passage, which would guarantee a 'good read' and sometimes, but not often, to save money. This is worth noting as it is not unusual to represent the modern reader as an someone who has neither the time, nor the inclination, to read any book more than once; the modern reader is, by definition, an extensive reader (Petrucci 1999:361). Having a copy of a favoured text allows the reader to re-visit, at will, a previously rewarding reading experience. In this vein, Eric told me that he preferred owning books to borrowing them from a library:

> because I like having something, it's the consumer in me I guess, I really like to take something with me and own it and feel like I possess it if you like, I like to

put it on my shelf and I like to leave it there afterwards because I like to go back
to my books (E).

Eric's desire to keep his books is similar to 'the thrill of acquisition' that,
writes Walter Benjamin, drives the collector of cultural artefacts (Benjamin
1992:62). More dramatically, George Steiner regards this desire to possess
books as a question of control: 'the whole question [of book ownership] is
one of the power relationship over this object' (Steiner 1973:18). Alternatively, collections of cultural objects, like books, may contribute to the self-
representation of the collector (Marks 1994; Muensterberger 1994; Windsor
1994).

For Georgina, physical book exchanges are ambiguous, caught it seems
between conflicting desires:

there is the nice idea that you're passing it on, you're passing on the knowledge ... I used to think like that you know, rounds of swapping books, but now
I'm very proud of my bookshelf [laughs] (G).

On the one hand, Georgina regards the exchange of books as good because
they constitute a particular stream in the flow of knowledge between people:
to swap books is to swap ideas. But, on the other hand, her book collection
suitably displayed is also of value. This tension between lending and displaying books could also be interpreted as a choice perhaps between two different modes of self-representation. Telling perhaps is Georgina's use of
'bookshelf', rather than book collection or just simply books. Bookshelves
and -cases constitute a spatialised record of reading in a way similar to that of
a trophy cabinet: the books are markers of cultural achievement, achieve-
ments of which a reader may be proud. Georgina's sense of pride challenges
Antonio Petrucci's claims that the new and allegedly chaotic order of reading
is reflected in the way in which books are stored. Dislodged from their sacred position in the library and 'special pieces of furniture' in the home,
Petrucci asserts, books share 'the fate of those of other objects, which are in
great part inexorably ephemeral' (Petrucci 1999:365). By drawing such a
crude line between a golden past in which books were sacred objects and a
colourless yet profane present in which they are dispensable commodities, it
is easy to overlook the fact that novels in particular have only recently been
worthy of either collection or display (Lovell 1987:50). Moreover, while it is
certainly the case that books have been de-sacralised—they share domestic
space with televisions, radios, computers and stereos—it would be wrong to
suggest that a more intimate mode of reading has rendered books 'ephemeral' for all contemporary readers.

Of the readers I interviewed in their homes, all had books on show—in
bookcases or on shelves—in the communal living areas, while others told
me that they had a stack of books on their bedside tables: 'you know the pile

beside the bed sort of thing' (M). This semi-public display of books may be interpreted as an indication that those readers want others to take note of the books that they have read and the fact they are readers. The clustering of similar objects emphasises the importance of the class of objects, rather than individual objects themselves (Riggins 1994:114): books in general are more significant in this context than particular texts. Indeed, displays of books are still presumed to have a high degree of symbolic value which is often played upon in news and current affairs television broadcasts. It is common, when interviewing an expert in a particular field—especially a legal practitioner or academic—to frame the speaker against a background of neatly shelved texts which gives a symbolic authority to what is being said. The degree to which such a technique is effective in persuading the audience of an individual's authority is, however, another matter.

As well as functioning as a marker of status, bookcases may also record a reader's journey through books: they provide a home for the traces of a reading history. As a frequent re-reader, Eric keeps all the books he receives:

> I would hate to let go of the book for some reason ... maybe because in sort of letting the book go I'm ... relinquishing any sort of memory of it maybe, you know? I feel I might forget about it, it's good to have it there (E).

The book collection acts as an anchor for the narratives that are crucial for the maintenance of self-identity—we are, partly, what we read. The surrender of a book, for Eric, seems to be the equivalent of relinquishing a memory. Despite his self-proclaimed consumerism Eric seems far more worried about losing the *memory* of the book than losing the book itself. This fear could be related to the fact that self-identities require self-narratives, and that books have a part to play in their construction. The most obvious examples of people's efforts to project themselves through narrative may be found in the maintenance of a diary or journal, or working through an autobiography (Giddens 1991:76). Other ways of self-projection, a little less obvious because they do not involve the act of writing, could include photograph albums, collections or family heirlooms that, among other uses, 'bear material witness to the age and continuity of the lineage' (Bourdieu 1984:76). As Roland Barthes indicates, photographs provide a consciousness of 'having been there' and, in so doing, they help to stabilise individual identities. This stabilisation is achieved through the creative linking of the present with the past in a process that resembles an act of remembering forwards (Barthes 1984:44). Readers may certainly use their book collections in a manner similar to a photograph album. A book may offer 'proof', not of 'having been there', as in the case of a photograph, but of 'having read that then' and of being 'the person who read that then'. The reader and the book, the reading subject and the read object, are articulated in time: in the 'memory-space'

(Wise 2000:298) or, as Vera Marks has argued, books may be 'memory objects' that open a space for remembering (Marks 1994:91).

In the process of reflexive development, self-identity is apprehended 'in relation to a given time and space' (Sarup 1996:15), so that '[t]he self has a coherence that derives from a cognitive awareness of the various phases of the lifespan' (Giddens 1991:75). The use of books to mark the trajectory of the 'lifespan' is made quite explicit by Vincent who, when asked to compare Toni Morrison's *Beloved* with other books he had read, changed the focus of the discussion:

> I don't know whether I'd compare it [*Beloved*] with other stuff in America ...
> coz it's more, it's more, more for me a book that I remember from a certain
> era, before going back to university ... part of a whole series of books I read
> about then (V).

Rather than provide possible analogues of Morrison's novel, as he was asked, Vincent uses the book to fix a particular period in his life: reading *Beloved* marked a particular autobiographical moment. A good example of a book's ability to operate as 'memory objects' was related by Natasha who explained candidly how she had used particular types of books as a means to cope with an unwanted pregnancy:

> I had a termination of a pregnancy [...] and to cope with it I had to wait until
> the days leading up to it, there was about a week where I couldn't get out of
> bed because I was so sick and ... what I wanted more than anything else, I
> didn't want to watch TV, I didn't want to read a book, I wanted to be read
> fairytales ... now how do you analyse that?

Having asked the rhetorical question, something of a dare, Natasha then proceeded to offer a complex and highly personal answer:

> That's really quite, it says a lot about how, I guess at that time I realised how
> much I used books as a young child to dissociate from my family and the
> dramas that were going on around me and I think that the fact that I didn't
> want to read just anything, I wanted specific fairytales and I had a book at my
> mother's house, that were really, really beautiful, there was some Isaac Asimov
> and like classic fairytales and some tales were set in knights and ladies times
> [laughs] medieval times and, yeah and they, I really needed it .... comfort, it
> made me feel like I [was] innocent and little again at that time (N).

In this moving account, books are used to mark three distinct stages in the life narrative: three different selves are articulated here. There is Natasha as the innocent fairytale-reading child; the young women dealing with a pregnancy and critically reflecting on her childhood, and as an older woman narrating her story in the context of a research interview. The association of reading fairytales with an 'innocent' period of her life allows Natasha to seek comfort from a former self. Although not always in such dramatic circumstances, books may be then used as external markers of particular points in the reflexive process of maintaining a self-identity, or of narrating a life story, that is by implication, also the fashioning of a social identity.

Talking books

Buckridge *et al* suggest that recreational reading—'reading which allowed time alone'—had replaced 'collective discovery and pleasure' for their group of readers (Buckridge *et al* 1995:9). 'Collective discovery', in this case, refers to periods of the interviewees' lives, most often school and university, where they shared their reading interests more readily with others similarly disposed. Certainly, reader Anthony spoke fondly of his brief time at university, and the opportunities he then had for 'collective discovery': 'I used to, up in Cairns, I used to love it, I'd talk to lecturers too, there's more, it's easier to contact your lecturer, it's a smaller uni, ... we'd sit in coffee shops [laughs] and talk about books' (A).

Although all the readers read more or less in such a 'recreational' manner, there remains a strong, if submerged, collective element to their reading practice. Books provide a site of common ground, a territory which provides a location for discussion—discussion is a significant form of interaction (O'Connor 1992:147). Just as book exchanges may constitute an opening of the self to the other, so may conversations: conversations 'enable an exteriorisation of the self' (Maffesoli 1996:25). Moreover, conversations create intersubjective moments that bind people to shared ideas or create a ground upon which they may disagree (Maffesoli 1996:25). Conversation is highly important to the development of reading communities owing to the nature of reading itself. Unlike some other leisure activities, reading is not generally undertaken in proximal groups. Therefore, direct interaction between readers is primarily talking about reading, rather than reading itself.

Consequently, as Virginia Nightingale explains, the relationship between the audience and the text extends past the moment of reading and viewing (Nightingale 1996:148); just as the broadcast text of television is overtaken by 'the performed text', so book talk continues the person's textual engagement beyond the act of reading itself. Ellen Seiter goes further, arguing that the act of talking about books, films or television programmes may sometimes be more important than the text being discussed because 'media talk is crucially related to the management of social relationships, engaged in as a means of maintaining social connections as much as it is motivated by interest in the media per se' (Seiter 1999:3). Through talk, including conversations about the media, cultural actors 'produce' their identities (Harrison

1998:102). Significantly, book talk is most often a form of symbolic exchange that relies on face-to-face contact. Hence, unlike other forms of exchange, book talk as a way of managing friendship does not extend a reader's funds of sociability.

Book discussion often takes the form of a reading recommendation. The following readers, Vincent, Georgina, Roz and Madelaine, all indicate that reading advice is a major constituent of their book talk:

> It always starts off with have you read? ... and then ... I just, just ... if you want to recommend it to people or you talk about why it was crap, why it was a waste of time, what you liked about it (V).

> *Do you recommend a lot of books to friends?*
> Yeah and vice versa (V).

> *Do you talk much about your reading?*
> Yeah I suppose I do, If you know I've read something [...] if I've read something I really like I'll usually sort of buy the same book for everyone's birthday [laughs] I like this book, you should like it too! ... yep if I really, really like something I'd talk about it, but it depends who I'm talking about it too (G).

> *Do you talk about your reading very much?*
> Only if I find a book that's absolutely wonderful so I have to tell everyone it and make them read it (R).

> *Why do you recommend books to people?*
> Coz, ... I like them [the person] and I think they should read it too and some-times coz I want somebody to read a book so I can say, talk about it and especially if that's a sort of, like a tricky book, a sneaky story, some description, so that you can say to some, when did you work it out? or you know what-ever, something like that, otherwise if people ask you, sometimes, what book's a good book?, or you know, it might come up in conversation people are talking about a book and you'd say I read so-and-so and it was good (M).

In Lana's reading community, discussions about books often result in the lending of a text: 'so my friends will all talk to me, and generally the end of the discussions means I lend the book to them, and they give it back to me and generally that goes on for a long time' (L). The frequency of recommen-dation by the readers contrasts with Buckridge *et al*'s observation that read-ing advice was, surprisingly to them, not a feature of their readers' practice: '[i]ndeed, the most striking and perhaps significant feature of this part of the second interview was the respondents' uniform lack of interest in the ques-tion of recommendations. It was simply not a question that had occurred to them, or that it engaged them once it was raised' (Buckridge, *et al* 1995:26).

The majority of the readers I spoke to said that they spoke with others about their reading. Book talk is not confined to the making of recommendations. Ivana, for example, told me that book talk deepened her knowledge: 'I like talking about books ... I like people to talk to me about books because I don't think I know enough' (I). Another reader, Dirk, described his book discussions in the following way:

> *Do you talk to people about your books?*
> with some people you know, a few people, you'd come across people with the same interest as you, being that there's so many books out there, occasionally when I do yes, I'll talk for hours with them about particular series or something like that (D).

Dirk seems to be highly selective in his book conversations, preferring long in-depth discussions with others who share his interest in 'particular series' of fantasy or science fiction novels. Dirk explained how his book exchanges were sometimes motivated by a desire to talk about his reading, 'it gives me someone to talk about it [the book] with ...' (D). As the books themselves seem to frame the debate, long conversations could only be possible with others who possess a similar amount of specific knowledge, a knowledge that Dirk apparently tries to cultivate. It is possible to draw an analogy between Dirk's preferred type of book discussion and the sorts of discourses that operate within a more specialised fan culture.

Dirk's selectivity, and his fan-like book talk, contrasts with Frances's more frequent and much broader discussions about books:

> because I live with my mum we often read the same books so we talk about a book after we've both read it and with my friends if we have all read the same book which is some pairs of us or whatever have read the book I quite often talk about it, and I tell my friends at work about the book that I've read, and what happened, if it was interesting, if it had some sort of relevance to what we were doing that day (F).

Frances explained the complex ways in which she talks about her reading. Her book conversations appear influenced by the social relationship within which they occur—one text can form the basis of quite different types of discussions:

> well ... with my work friends I would tell them an anecdote from the book more or less like something that had one little part of the book like a story in itself, like I read a book and this happened blah blah and it sort of has ... the whole thing within it, it's like telling the story without telling the whole book, with my friends and my Mum probably we'd talk about how bits you'd liked and how it affected you emotionally and something else, I don't know, you'd say I was really scared when I read the bit that said this, or didn't this bit seem like your own life or something like that (F).

Not surprisingly, Frances's discussions about books with her friends and family are far more intimate, more self-revealing, than those with her work colleagues. Her description is couched in lay, rather than technical, language.

Although the discussions draw on the resources of a 'social', rather than a 'serious' reader (Becker 1982), Frances speaks about books through numerous discourses. She speaks of the narrative of the text, gives synopses, preferences, comments on a novel's emotional affect and the intersection of the text with her own life narrative.

Book talk may depend on the context of the discussion, the social relationship between the participants being just one example. However, the book itself also contributes to the discursive parameters; the text is a context:

> Yeah depends on the person you're talking too and the book, I mean if the book's just a lightweight non-intense book you might say about the funny things that happened or whatever and then if there were like … some books are more intense they have more bearing … on your emotions … and how you related to the book even though I hate that term related because I mean, it's not your auntie [laughs] it's a book, but anyway, connected or something, so you know it varies on the book and the person (F).

Frances's commentary upon her own practices outlines the relationship between the type of book and her own discussions: a 'lightweight non-intense book' produces humour while something 'more intense' would have a very different effect. In the following chapter, I will look more closely at the textual economy of everyday readership: the manner in which texts frame reading performance.

Just as readers match books to potential readers, so conversations about books take place within the context of the readers' interests:

> I talk to my flatmate about books, [she] and I tend to both like books written by women of a certain era so I say, I don't talk about the cyberpunk aspect of my reading, she's not interested in that, but I've got another friend who is … (L).

> I normally talk about things that I know that the person will find interesting, I remember talking about *Beloved* actually, and trying to get my friend Julie to read it and saying … that even though … it was on *Oprah* … it's still a good book, read it it's really good [laughs] and talking about the gothic bits coz I know she likes gothic stuff and … whatever her personality traits fit with the book (R).

In both these cases, the readers talk about books in ways that they think will be interesting to their interlocutor. In the second extract, Roz not only recommends *Beloved*, she goes further by re-interpreting the novel in a way she thinks will appeal to the potential reader: her friend Julie likes 'gothic stuff' so Roz speaks of 'the gothic bits' and, consequently, in the context of the conversation, *Beloved* is made into a gothic novel. Roz's ability to 'turn' *Beloved* into a gothic novel is predicated on her own, and her friend's, knowledge of the formal elements of the gothic genre. The interpretative act moves from the consideration of a text, to a genre, and then on to the interpretation of a person: there are multiple acts of interpretation transacted in this type of encounter.

Book talk takes different forms depending on the reader, the type of book and the social relationship within which the conversation takes place. Here, Eric tells me of his book discussions with his father:

> ... dad and I probably have huge conversations about different books ... ... and huge, huge arguments about books.
> *And what sort of things would you talk about in those book talks?*
> Ah ... we talk about, particularly in science fiction we'd talk about the content ... ... and the plausibility of the premise I'd guess ... I guess we'd both see science fiction as being a vision of tomorrow, a philosophy so ... yeah we'd speak about that a lot ... we also argue about the value of different books, the value of literature (E).

It is the philosophical content, rather than the style or form, of science fiction novels that contributes most to Eric and his father's book talk. Eric places emphasis on the consensual nature of their conversations, exemplified through their common definition of science fiction writing as 'a vision of tomorrow, a philosophy', while also making it clear that books are the subject of disagreement: 'we also argue about the value of different books' (E). Consensus and dissonance are then both features of this particular reading community. Even though proto-communities, as 'taste cultures', are united by a shared interest, this does not seem to preclude disagreement. Such dissent may indeed reinforce, rather than undermine, reading communities. The more readers have invested in their practices, the more they may be inclined to defend them. Moreover, disagreement could also operate as a means to individuate particular social actors within particular communities.

The degree to which book discussions may be influenced by education is indicated by Winston's reading proto-community. His and his friends' book talk is heavily informed by a shared university background. Unlike Frances's book discourse, which is highly personalised, Winston and his reading friends have discussions that are reminiscent of 'tutorials':

> I've got friends who I did [uni] with ... and it's, it's just what we do we talk about books and about ideas [...] but in a way we've been accustomed, trained to, you know, how does this book fit into this genre, how does it relate to this book and this makes me think of that play, and what's the connection there so yeah but not I love this book and this book speaks about my life, although that's always part of what we do anyway. [...] These are ongoing things like we develop, we say you remember that conversation we had about James' *Ambassadors* and you said that and I said this but now how does that fit so it's an ongoing thing, the type of discussion you'd have in tutorials (W).

He and his friends take the discourses learned in tertiary study and deploy them in a more generalised social situation. Winston expresses an awareness of the effects of his tertiary education on his book talk by making a non-judgemental comparison between his book discussions based on literary discourse and those driven by a more autobiographical agenda. The shared knowledge of 'literary' ways of speaking about books is the product of mutual experience; conversations that invoke the shared experience afford a sense of cohesion and continuity for those concerned: 'that's what *we* do anyway' (W, his emphasis).

The differences between Frances's and Winston's reading practices may be seen as cultural performances determined simply by different forms of cultural capital. Melissa uses 'everyday' discourses in her book discussions, discourses that are 'based on the affirmation of continuity between art and life' (Bourdieu 1984:32). In contrast, Winston's conscious interest in intertextuality is commensurate with an 'aesthetic disposition' that constitutes a break from everyday attitudes towards the relationship between expressive forms and the world. Frances's book talk is part of a popular aesthetic that stresses a popular taste based on 'recognition' of what is represented, while Winston's may seem to assert the 'primacy of form over function' (Bourdieu 1984:32), where representation is more significant than what is represented. The difference between these discourses becomes a marker for both cultural and social distinction.

As Bourdieu would argue, the foundation for this ability to discriminate 'correctly' is the product of a particular type of aesthetic education. However, within the context of this study, a simple correlation between readers' book discourse and their level of education is not maintained: an 'aesthetic education' does not seem to dictate, automatically, the nature of book discussions. Belinda—who holds a humanities degree—discusses books with her friends in a manner similar to that of Frances. She might talk:

> about which is a good book is, you know, if they've read a good book they might mention it and I might mention a good book or if I'm reading a book I might discuss details of the book and how it impacted on me or something like that (B).

Like Belinda and Frances, Karen also links her reading, through discussion, with her every day life experiences:

> *What are the things you are likely to talk about, about a book?*
> I don't know maybe it would be about how it impacted on me, or how it affected me ... (K).

Unlike Frances and Belinda, however, Karen then proceeds to broaden the interview with this significant comment:

... I don't think I generally talk about like how a book was, how well it was
written or, you know, all that, it would be more about what impact it had on
me I suppose (K).

Karen indicates that while she is aware of other ways of talking about books,
ways that may be more 'legitimate', they do not readily fall within the parameters of her own book discourse, which appears to stress the affective
qualities of a text. The particular way in which readers talk about books may
be as much the product of the reading proto-communities in which their
book discussions circulate, as it is their own individual levels of education.
Frances and Winston's book talk is the product of both education *and* membership of particular reading proto-communities. Knowledge of more 'legitimate' registers of cultural discourse may not be deployable within particular
social networks that value books in different ways. So, while being able to
speak about 'intertextuality' may be a sign of cultural distinction within some
reading communities, in others it may have little purchase. Karen may know
how to discuss novels in terms of their formal properties, she may possess
knowledge of certain literary discourses, but she may not actually deploy
these during discussions within the socio-cultural network in which she exchanges books. In such a situation, the ability to use 'aesthetic discourse'
may still operate as a mark of otherness, but not necessarily legitimacy.

Possession of an aesthetic education, *in itself*, does not appear then to
crudely determine the substance of readers' book talk. From the opposite
perspective, however, some of the readers without an aesthetic education
demonstrate a complex understanding of form as well as content, even when
they express their awareness in more general language. Readers' comments
seem to suggest that their reading practices run counter to Bourdieu's 'popular aesthetic'. Cultural consumers—even without 'legitimate' cultural capital—may be well aware of the differences between the diegetic world of the
narrative and their own lives (Jenkins 1992:66; Willis 1990:33). Genre, for
instance, is not just the concern of academic institutions and their discourses,
as the example of reader's use of generic knowledge of 'the gothic' shows.
Knowledge of a particular cultural form is available from many places, not
just through formal education. This is significant, considering that the vast
majority of the population does not acquire, in any formal sense, a cultural
education beyond secondary school. As Raymond Williams has suggested,
expressive forms are shared commodities in which writers, cultural industries, academics and readers all have a large investment (Williams 1977:187).
Readers in this study are generally capable of discussing both content and
form. This is quite clearly demonstrated by Terri who discusses: 'the language, the plot, the story, what we know about the author, the bits we love,
what we got from it' with other members of her reading community (T).

In stressing the frequency and abundance of book talk as a form of symbolic exchange among the readers, there is a tendency to overlook those readers for whom book talk is not a way to be sociable. So, while Julie exchanges books in other ways (recommendations, presents), discussions about books are not a feature of her reading practice which 'is very solitary' (J). The other 'non-talker', Madelaine, goes further and actually tries to avoid conversing about books:

> *Do you discuss the books you read with others?*
> Not much, I have always avoided studying literature ... Reading has always had a bit of a magical quality for me, I was, am somewhat afraid that too much theorising, discussion, analysis would cause me to lose that magic (M).

From her comments it seems that Madelaine may have interpreted my question about book discussions in terms of academic modes of reading. She equates book discussions with 'theorising' and 'analysis', ways of reading texts that may demystify or dispel the 'magical quality' that she attribute to her reading. Although she is sometimes drawn into book discussions with her mother as they tend to read the same books, she makes certain that it's 'nothing too deep though' (M).

Finally, a third type of reader, who is also very much in the minority, claims not to have sufficient opportunities in which to talk about her or his reading. In the following extract, Zoe speaks of her efforts to talk about her books:

> ... I try like [talk to] my flatmate's really good coz we often read the same stuff ... ... and I [laughs] I find myself bringing stuff up all the time but people sort of switch off so [laughs] you know it's just silly.
> *So you'd like to be able to talk about your reading?*
> Yes ... I think it is a really relevant point, it comes into the conversation, I think it is really relevant but they don't care because it's just fiction (Z).

Zoe here makes the comparison between successful book discussions with her flatmate, who is within her reading community, and the less favourable responses of outsiders. Lana makes a similar point in a different way: 'people tend to start looking extremely bored when a book person discusses [puts on a different voice] "my latest book"' (L). It is important to remember that any individual social actor is always embroiled in a number of overlapping, intersecting or even separate proto-communities simultaneously. As in Zoe's commentary above, the social interaction generated through the material and symbolic exchange of books within one specific community may not be transferable to another. In this situation socio-cultural networks lose the largely positive aspect that I have so far assigned to them and become restrictive; they involve 'coercion and exclusion, and can be normative and controlling' (Long 1987:16).

Whose values?

Peter Mann argues that 'the book as a gift is an interesting phenomenon, since it is acknowledged that ownership of books confers status, and therefore, to give books as presents is also a status-conferring action' (Mann 1971:53). Mann is, however, unclear as to the values that book exchanges actually symbolise. I have suggested that proto-communities, in a general sense, are not determined simply by class interests. However, the overwhelmingly middle-class socio-economic backgrounds of the readers in this study needs to be considered.

The relatively small size of the sample of readers makes any quantitative generalisation about the social class status of novel-reading dangerous. However, it may be possible to suggest that novel-reading, rather than another cultural practice, becomes the vehicle for personal relationships because reading novels is often associated with middle-class cultural values that valorise books and book-learning. So, from this perspective, the social economy of reading outlined in this chapter is one in which middle-class readers exchange books with other middle-class readers as tokens of cultural and social symmetry. In this regard Patricia O'Connor notes that 'friendships reflect and reinforce the stratified nature of the society, with friends typically being made with people from the same class, race, educational background, level of income, recreational interests etc.'(O'Connor 1998:110).

Some of the readers themselves seem to be aware partially of the relationship between social status and their reading. For example, Eric, who has a liking for canonical writers, suggests that his recent book choices—*The Glass Bead Game* (Hesse) and *A Portrait of the Artist as a Young Man* (Joyce)—are 'influenced by my middle-class pretension actually [laughs]'. When asked if he feels obliged to read 'literature', he replied: 'In a way there is definitely a stupid notion that they [literary texts] are more valuable than science fiction, perhaps I could read in my own bubble' (E). Another reader, Georgina, spoke of her 'middle-class upbringing' which included parental pressure to read novels (G). Unsurprisingly, such an ideological function of book exchanges is not featured in most readers' own discourse because, as Becker suggests, 'people do not experience their aesthetic beliefs as merely arbitrary and conventional; they feel they are natural, proper and moral' (cited in Bennett *et al* 1999:8). For my readers, book exchanges do certainly have a 'status-conferring' function, but a function that is consciously aligned with the maintenance of relationships rather than in the reproduction of particular values. But to maintain an absolute differentiation between 'the personal' and 'the cultural' is not possible. To do so would be to suggest that personal identity exists beyond the borders of the cultural realm.

The apparent symmetry between social status and cultural practice could be the product of received ideas about the nature of the novel and its readership. Novel reading is not, and never has been, an exclusively middle-class activity even if the novel as a cultural form has been used, during some historical periods, to establish middle-class cultural hegemony. To see the novel as an unproblematic and ahistorically middle-class cultural interest ignores the complicated relation between the two. Cavallo and Chartier are critical of approaches that fail to realise 'that cultural differentiation is not necessarily organised according to the one grid of social status as the controlling factor in an unequal distribution or variations in practices' (Cavallo and Chartier 1999:4). As a cultural form the novel has moved up Stuart Hall's 'cultural escalator'; from its status as a middle-class 'popular' entertainment in the eighteenth century to a position as art-object in the twentieth: Leavis's 'Great Tradition' was primarily one of novelists (Leavis 1948). Although often read by a predominately middle-class audience, the novel has not always been a machine for generating bourgeois hegemony. Jonathan Rose (2001) shows, for example, how novels were used by working-class readers as a means of self- and sometimes radical education. Readers, along with writers, publishers, teachers and academics, have at various times used the novel as a medium for the criticism of those normative middle-class cultural and social values.

Finally, the correlation between socio-economic class and novel-reading may also be influenced by the research project itself. Reading fiction is the centre of the study but it is not the only cultural activity in which the readers engage. Books are a feature of the readers' cultural and social lives, but so is listening to recorded music, watching television, playing musical instruments, sport (both participation and spectatorship), going to the cinema and bushwalking. Another study of the same group, using a different cultural practice or medium, could uncover other consumption patterns and affiliations to numerous proto-communities which would, in turn, lead to other conclusions being drawn. This is demonstrated well by Vincent, a university lecturer who is both a reader of literary fiction *and* a compulsive viewer of the reality-television programme *Popstars* (V). Vincent's cultural tastes could be used to both support and disrupt stable notions of 'class culture'. Indeed after interviewing the middle-class readers for this study, it is much harder to state what the cultural values of book readers actually are in any totalising sense, other than the fact that they value reading.

Conclusion

Harold Bloom is right to make the connection between books and friends, but, in claiming that reading constitutes a turning away from the social, he seems to ignore the social economy of reading as it functions within the culture of readers like those interviewed for this book. Like the spatio-temporal economy of everyday reading, the social economy within which my readers operate is invisible to formalist methods of cultural analysis. Social networks are a significant cultural resource in the material sense that they are the primary source of books in both a symbolic and material sense. This exchange of books also provides a form of sociality that is not always dependent on frequent physical proximity because, just as finding 'free time' to read is difficult, so is the opportunity to maintain social contact. Therefore, book exchanges increase a reader's 'funds of sociability' and provide a means to manage and maintain relationships beyond face-to-face contact. The success of a book exchange may act as an index of intimacy and, whether exchanged or semi-publicly displayed, books are embroiled in the process of identity formation: books in this context have both an instrumental and an expressive use-value. Rather than constitute a retreat from the social and a move toward 'otherness' (Bloom 2001), the social economy of everyday reading draws cultural actors into webs of sociality. In this fashion, book exchanges become a way of embedding social relationships through the shared consumption of cultural commodities.

Note

1.   See also Joshua Meyrowitz, *No Sense of Place: The Impact of Electronic Media on Social Behaviour* (1988), for a detailed discussion of the post-print media's erosion of the relationship between physical location and identity (Meyrowitz 1988:143).

4   'A Lot of Morrison's Stuff Is Sad': Readers, Repertoires, Texts

> Reading texts is a matter of reading them in the light of other texts, people, obsessions, bits of information, or what have you, and then seeing what happens.
>
> *Richard Rorty*, The Pragmatist's Progress

> What would reading lives be like if they weren't preoccupied with, or nagged by, the dream of literature? In such a world the reader who finds Toni Morrison a hectoring drag and Salman Rushdie a radical-chic blowhard wouldn't hesitate to say so.
>
> *Ray Sawhill*, Unrequired Reading

Introduction

Up to this point, I have concentrated on what we might call the extra-textual dimension of everyday reading, in an attempt to map the reading, meanings and uses of books that operate outside the text-as-narrative. In doing so, I have not as yet considered the books that my informants actually read. While I certainly agree with Ien Ang that the significance of a cultural object 'cannot be decided upon outside of the multidimensional intersubjective networks in which the object is inserted' (Ang 1996:70), this accent on the contexts of consumption does not mean that the texts themselves have no role to play in this process. After all, readers read books, not 'intersubjective networks'. To my mind, denying the materiality of the book erases the creative discriminations that people bring to their reading. All the readers I interviewed expressed, often quite passionately, their preferences for particular books, authors or genres over others. To erase the text from everyday reading would be to omit a certain manifest quality of everyday reading culture. This chapter, therefore, returns to the text and examines how readers use their limited interpretative resources, or 'repertoires' (Hermes 1995), to make sense of a particular narrative within the field of everyday cultural consumption. The narrative I have chosen is a novel by the well-known and often controversial African-American writer Toni Morrison.

Remember the text?

Even if we no longer regard them as discrete and autonomous objects, cultural texts still play a constituent role in the practices of cultural actors and, in turn, the social realm that is shaped, and gives shape to those practices. Texts have 'objective possibilities', which Willis defines as 'internal structures' that are 'capable of bearing a broad but theoretically finite range of potential meanings' (Willis 2001:109). These structures circumscribe the way in which that text may be used. The production of texts, and of meanings, is therefore 'an exercise in delimitation' (Corner 1983:280). While books may not have a single, fixed, formally determined meaning, neither do they mean absolutely anything: 'even for the most resisting reader, it is actually quite difficult to laugh at *Schindler's Ark*' (Milner 2005:185). In this sense it is possible to speak of an economy of the text: the ability of the narrative to support certain readings but to undermine others, dependent upon the cultural competencies and contextualities of the readership; this confluence of forces constitutes an everyday economy of the text, the focus of this chapter.

Having reiterated the importance of particular books in everyday practices, it is important to select an appropriate text to reveal the operation of the textual economy of reading. On face value, a novel by a Nobel Laureate may appear an odd choice for the study of an everyday economy of the text.

Which book? Choosing a case study

As I suggested in an earlier chapter, mass-mediated texts have frequently been scrutinised through the application of literary and cultural theories, themselves originating from within aesthetic institutions. By selecting Toni Morrison's *Beloved* as a case study the polarity of this particular academic operation is reversed; a novel that is firmly ensconced within the academy as high art is analysed in the context of an everyday readership. *Beloved* is, after all, available to everyday consumption in the same way that the animated satire *The Simpsons* or *Batman* graphic novels are accessible to academic or aesthetic discourse. From the perspective of the institutional reading, looking at canonical texts as they are read informally and unprofessionally is an exercise in defamiliarisation.

Morrison's novel was also chosen to avoid organised fandom. A great deal of research has been conducted into the operation and significance of quasi-official fan communities (Jenkins 1992; Lewis 1992; Cavicchi 1998). Cultural studies' widespread and continued interest in fan cultures is akin to sociology's obsession with 'nuts, sluts and perverts' (Hammersley 1992:25). Fan cultures, like 'deviant' subcultures, are attractive to researchers because such interpretative communities seem to provide a discrete location for formal ethnographic activity. Book clubs, 'alternative' music venues, various urban tribes and fanzines alike appear as relatively still places in the whirling complexity and thorough interconnectedness of everyday life in western media cultures. In reality, however, the vast majority of cultural consumption takes place outside such semi-formal organisations and, as a result of cultural and media studies' concentration on fandom, such media use is overlooked (Hermes 1995:148).

The selection of *Beloved* is further prompted by the complex nature of Morrison and her novel's cultural location. Significantly, a novel like *Beloved* problematises the high/low cultural binary, exemplifying instead a mass-produced text that occupies multiple and, supposedly, for those arbiters of taste, contradictory positions within the socio-cultural world. From one position, Morrison is indisputably a 'literary writer', a Pulitzer Prize-winner and the first American-born writer since John Steinbeck to become a Nobel Laureate. Within an academic environment, Morrison's narratives of black experience are read within the traditions of American, African-American, feminist, Black feminist, and Southern literature, and within literary theoretical discourses such as psychoanalysis, Marxism and post-colonialism. *Beloved* is the book which 'secured Morrison's reputation'; evidence for the high academic reputation the book enjoys is indicated by the MLA bibliography which contains over 400 post-*Beloved* entries (Plasa 2000:6). Alongside Morrison-as-literary-author is Morrison the civil rights activist who has used her celebrity to speak out on race and gender issues such as the Clarence Thomas-Anita Hill hearings of 1991,[1] and to voice her conspicuous support for O.J. Simpson in 1995.[2] Linking the pedagogical with the political, Morrison's books are read as interventions in racial and gender histories and politics.

Beyond but not disconnected from art and politics is Morrison as media celebrity and bestselling author. The increasingly celebrity of 'African American authors like Toni Morrison shows how simple questions of market appeal can merge with broader social, cultural and racially inflected issues' (Moran 2000:50). There is an indication that she had a popular following before she attracted mainstream academic attention. Her status as literary celebrity is demonstrated by her involvement in Oprah Winfrey's networked daytime television programme, *The Oprah Winfrey Show*, and the moribund 'Oprah's Book Club'. Morrison's television appearances raised her profile to such an extent that *Beloved*, although never an official Book Club selection, sold 900,000 copies in America within two weeks of her engagement on Winfrey's programme. The American Literacy Society reported that these sales equated to twice the number of Morrison's total sales for the previous 20 years (Jackman 1999:57). This stunning figure could be inflated considering that, according to another source, *Song of Solomon* (1977) alone sold 570,000 copies

(David 2000:19). But even if the sales of *Beloved* were less than the 900,000 claimed, there still appears to be a large number of Morrison novels in general circulation. *Beloved's* initial American print run of 100,000 copies (in autumn 1987) suggests that the publishers, Knopf, scheduled the book for a broad appeal; the novel was also a 'main selection' for the Book-of-the-Month-Club (Donaghue 1987: electronic source). The assumption that there is a considerable general readership for Morrison's novels is also indicated by the publication of *Toni Morrison Explained: A Reader's Road Map to the Novels*, a book 'that would give anyone, regardless of age or education, everything they needed to understand and enjoy Toni Morrison's novels' (David 2000:vii). In summary, I envisaged Morrison's novel as a possible literary analogue of *Carmina Burana*. Like Orff's composition, Morrison and her novels, as indeed all cultural commodities, are available for multiple *re-articulations*.

In my attempt to apprehend a particular, everyday textual reading economy, the overall purpose of this book becomes more than a little vulnerable. By asking questions that direct the reader's attention towards the narrative understanding of a particular book there is perhaps a risk that I will impose a more academic textual practice upon the informants than they themselves exercise: one economy of the text could overwrite another. Batsleer *et al* warn of the dangers that arise from asking questions in search of a single authoritative meaning in, or of, a text (Batsleer *et al* 1985:147). In their demands for direct answers to straightforward questions ('What about the ending? What do you think of this character? Is it realistic?'), the researchers 'found that we were once more elevating the texts above the social relations and practical circumstances within which they exist and which give them meaning' (ibid.). The textual economy of reading professionals diverges from that of everyday cultural consumers and, therefore, questions researchers think significant and insightful may miss completely the everyday significance, or otherwise, of a particular book.

Aware of the dangers of imposing an academic regime of value on the readers, I tried to avoid the types of questions that Batsleer *et al* counsel against. But despite this intention I did on a few occasions, inadvertently, ask a question about the meaning of the novel in such a direct manner and when I did so, I found the question did not stimulate a great deal of interest on the readers' behalf. Readers' answers to such a direct assault were brief, often taking the form of a list: 'America, familial dislocation, legacies of slavery.' (V), or sometimes just a simple reply like this from Zoe: '[laughs] I don't know [laughs] I don't know, like ...' (Z). Not satisfied with giving such an answer, Zoe went further and actually challenged the validity of my question. She told me that there was a lot more to *Beloved* than its narrative meaning:

a lot of it is more the imagery, the sound, you're meant to say it aloud, yeah I don't think it's meant to be, I don't think you are meant to decipher it and learn what it means because then you lose everything I think (Z).

Zoe here is advocating a way of reading that rejects the hermeneutic tradition. It would be interesting to speculate on the origins of such an approach because this non-hermeneutic technique is generally not a reading praxis encouraged by educational institutions.

Such inquisitorial lapses aside, I inquired about the readers' impressions of *Beloved* in broad terms and attempted, not always with complete success, to avoid using literary discourse. Despite this, looking across the breadth of the interviews, it would seem that the interviewees were, perhaps not unsurprisingly, far more comfortable engaging with questions related to the social context of their reading. While answers to questions such as 'where do you read?' were answered at ease and at length, it was much harder to get the readers to speak about *Beloved*, as a text, in great detail.

There are two obvious reasons for this contrast: the nature of everyday readership and the nature of memory. Although they may or have had 'professional' relationships with other texts, the readers did not possess a large number of specialised discourses through which to articulate anything approaching a comprehensive explanation of the narrative meaning(s) of *Beloved*. As a result, as an interviewer I was often left with a choice between asking increasingly direct and leading questions about the book, in order to facilitate responses that would supply more 'useful' information about the novel, data that was more legitimate within academic domains, or moving on to another question or topic area: most often I inclined towards the latter position.

Similarly, memory also plays a major part in research interviews. In analysing readers' responses to questions, the effect of the passage of time must be considered. Retrospective questions in a qualitative research context are problematic because memories, produced as they are in the interstices between past and present, are fundamentally unreliable. Reading is practised daily but a particular book might be 'performed' only once, therefore talking about the practice of reading as a activity is easier because it is commonplace; most of the people I interviewed were closer to the practice than they were to any one reading of a specific book. Readers were asked, in effect, to remember and narrate their reading of a particular book, to reconstruct their feelings, opinions and evaluations, and while some readers had read the novel recently, in one case only the day before the interview, most had read *Beloved* some months before. Even though I did not suggest that they needed to re-read the book before the interview, a few readers did so, feeling that they needed to re-familiarise themselves with the novel in order to be 'good' interviewees; they did not want to rely on memory, nor appear ill-informed. In no small way, the double-time filters of memory (Luisa Passerini cited in Taksa and Lyons 1992:14) make a contribution to the uneven and sometimes contradictory views that are expressed in many ethnographic interviews.

Expectations

The readers' memories were tested throughout the interview, not least when I asked them to relate their expectations prior to reading Morrison's novel. Expectations are important because they constitute part of the impetus to obtain and read a particular text and contribute to the pleasure that readers take from their reading. Through expectations and reflections the text is transformed into an experience (Iser 1988:214-215) and subversion of expectations might even be one of the reading's pleasures (Rorty 2002). As a catalyst for interpretative framings, expectations allow readers to begin making sense of a book even before they begin reading. In his pioneering study in the 1920s, I.A. Richards was, in one sense, looking at the effect of expectations on reading practices. His students' analyses of the poems took place without the expectations that an author's name, and associated discourses, bring to a particular reading act (Milner 2005:185).

The readers seemed to have varied expectations of Morrison's novel, centred on two general considerations. First, they wondered about the quality of the reading experience that the particular book would provide: 'is the book a good or bad read?' and second, they had an expectation as to the content of the novel: 'what will the book be about?' It is apparent that these expectations are not necessarily mutually exclusive although this may sometimes be the case. The readers in general told me that they enjoyed reading *Beloved*, even though they seem often surprised or confused by its form and content.

Despite having little knowledge of the book, or its writer, the readers still had expectations. This is partly because the book was often recommended to them by a reading friend: 'my friend who works at Picador gave it to me and told me I had to read it' (V). Madelaine, in contrast, discovered the book for herself and based on her experiences of reading other Morrison novels, she was expecting an intense reading experience: 'I thought it might be sad. A lot of Toni Morrison stuff is sad' (M). Other readers' expectations were, by their own admission, much less accurate. Frances did not really know what to expect, but the book's content nonetheless came as a surprise: 'well I just didn't think it would be like it was yes [laughs], I didn't think it would actually be quite as supernatural, [...] the ghost element was a surprise because you don't read a great deal of books like that' (F). Overall, her experience of reading *Beloved* was better than she had anticipated: 'well I read the front of the book, the other books that she had written and things and that sort of put me off the book actually, because just the names of things, there's one called something "In the hood", or something and that always makes me go um and I don't want to read it' (F). Although perturbed by Morrison's publication list she told me that 'I read it [*Beloved*] and I thought it seems better than those [other books] sounded' (F). Julie, like a number of the other readers, told me that she felt she had misjudged the book: 'I thought it was going to be romantic, I thought it was going to be a romance story' and 'if you read the jacket or the back or the back of the cover, I don't think that it really prepares you for what's, what's inside the book' (J). The plot summary that appears on the cover of the Vintage edition seems to be the cause of Julie's initial and false expectation:

> It is the mid 1800s. At Sweet Home in Kentucky, an era is ending as slavery comes under attack from the Abolitionists. The worlds of Halle and Paul D. are to be destroyed in a cataclysm of torment and agony. The world of Sethe, however, is to turn from one of love to one of violence and death: the death of Sethe's baby daughter Beloved, whose name is the single world on the tombstone, who died at her mother's hands, and who will return to claim retribution (1997, Vintage edition: back cover).

Such a synopsis is not dissimilar to the plot descriptions that often accompany historical romances, its melodramatic tone clashes with the literary testimony that brackets it: Margaret Atwood describes the novel as a monument to Morrison's 'stature as a pre-eminent American novelist'; A.S. Byatt claims that *Beloved* is 'an American masterpiece'. Julie's discovery of the book through the connection with Oprah Winfrey may have also influenced her romantic expectations. Stereotypically, romances are the type of fiction most likely to be promoted to a predominantly female readership. Any close examination of the novels chosen for inclusion in Winfrey's programme would, however, act as a corrective to such expectations.

In a similar way, Belinda's assumptions about the book were, in her view, wide of the mark:

> I didn't expect it to be so, I don't know, I guess the experience of the book was something quite outside anything I would have experience of, or conceive that I could experience, so I didn't expect it to be so, to be quite as distant from my own ability to relate to it (B).

For this reader, the novel's diegetic world offers a reality that is unassimilable, a situation that should perhaps be expected. If part of a reader's practice is to relate her or his own experiences to those represented in the text then, for a contemporary white, middle-class, female Australian reader, narratives of slavery will, in some sense, always be 'outside' her experience. Belinda's apparent inability to 'relate' challenges the humanist assertion that texts are transparent, and that the novel—dealing as it is claimed with universal human concerns—is always assimilable to anyone who can read. Reading *Beloved* results in Belinda feeling 'distant' from her 'own ability to relate to it'. What is 'made strange' is then not so much the relationship between the text and the social world, but the reader's relationship with her own normally unquestioned reading practices.

Readers' expectations are tested by the novel's content, but they are also troubled by its form. This concern with form is voiced by this reader: 'I guess well she's a Pulitzer Prize-winning author and a Nobel Laureate, yes I was surprised by the lightness [of the novel]' (W). 'Lightness' is not an adjective that any other reader applied to Morrison's work, and perhaps not one that would readily be applied to any narrative concerned with slavery and infanticide. As Winston, perhaps feeling he needs to define his terms, went on to explain:

> what do I mean like lightness? I was expecting it to be much darker and much more, less of that magic-realism, and I guess because I have an idea of her as being very serious and very, being an intellectual and that kind of thing, so I was surprised but not disappointed (W).

The reader's expectations are undone by the lack of congruity between the nature of the subject matter, the use of a particular form and the reader's idea of the author. The image of the author bears heavily upon Winston's reading, an image that is far more severe, from his perspective, than the narrative itself. Implicit in this comment is the value judgement that magic-realism is a non-serious, or least a less serious, genre of writing. A writer with Morrison's *gravitas* should, presumably, have written in a more appropriate form. Such an opinion is predicated on Winston's use of literary discourses that aim to create and maintain the hierarchy of forms, genres and values.

Impressions: a difficult book

As a group, my informants had a favourable response to *Beloved* despite their sometimes unfulfilled expectations. Richard Rorty claims persuasively that emotional responses to books—readers' loves and hates—may be a more significant than 'respectful' or cerebral approaches to meaning. 'For a great love or a great loathing,' suggests Rorty, 'is the sort of thing that changes us by changing our purposes, changing the uses to which we shall put people and things and texts we encounter later' (Rorty 1992:107). The readers spoke about how the novel's style and structure contributed to their enjoyment. For example, Susan told me that: 'her writing. I just thought, as I said it was hard but she is the most beautiful writer, don't ask me why' and her writing is 'well made, [...] each word is perfect and the actual story itself was totally powerful and complex' (S). Vincent summed up the readers' feelings accurately when he explained that Morrison was 'a taxing writer' (V). Ultimately though it was not the difficulty of the book nor the rich texture of the language that impressed him, but the story itself: 'it had a pretty gripping story and it was, I did find it intensely moving, it's hard for me to remember exactly how I felt actually ... I think at the time I was quite blown away by it. I don't think I'd read anything like it [...] to be honest it was just the story, that sense of inevitable disclosure of something absolutely horrible, it grips you' (V).

Some readers found the novel difficult for reasons other than style and form. Winston, prepared for the difficult nature of Morrison's prose by his tertiary education, thought the book was hard in a different way: 'but as I say all the implications and themes—that was challenging, so it wasn't hard to read but it was hard to make sense of the experience after the fact. You couldn't just read it and not think about it afterwards' (W). The book was difficult because the content was hard to assimilate: 'I was puzzled by it, there was a lot to be puzzled by' (W). The theme of difficulty was raised by almost all readers. In contrast to Winston, who unequivocally seems to have situated the novel's difficulty at the level of content and ideas, Roz was far less clear in her opinion:

> I was instantly engaged in it, which is funny because I tried to get other people to read it and they read like half a chapter, the first chapter and said 'no this is too hard I can't concentrate on it' and I thought is it really that hard? and I read it again, I went straight into it, totally in and there was no way I was gunna put this book down, so I just can't understand people who find it hard at all, it's really strange.
> *Why do you think they find it hard?*
> Because they don't make the effort I suppose, or they're just not interested in that form of writing, maybe they've got different ideas how something should be written, maybe they just watch too much TV (R).

In this interview extract, Roz contrasts her reading of *Beloved* with the aborted attempts made by her friends. Roz seems to be criticising the other readers; it is their reading deficiencies that make *Beloved* difficult to read, rather than the novel being difficult itself. The novel is challenging, difficult or impossible to read, because her friends are lazy, possess a different sensibility, or just watch 'too much television'. Yet she also implies that the novel is indeed an inherently difficult one and that her ability to read it not once but twice is a mark of cultural distinction. Roz's pride was spelled out elsewhere in the interview when she told me: 'I got a kick out of reading it [*Beloved*] because I knew lots of other people couldn't' (R). There is little doubt here that Roz uses her reading to differentiate herself from her friends. From her comment this sense of separation could be made both in terms of taste and competency. The relation between difficulty and cultural competency is also suggested by Anthony who found the novel demanding: 'because I hadn't read for a while, it was hard to get into reading again. But I think only because of that' (A). In Anthony's case, his difficulty in reading the novel was the product neither of the book's formal properties nor in its thematic preoccupations, but a lack of reading practice.

In response to *Beloved*'s complexity one reader used an eccentric reading strategy. Although Julie told me that she 'couldn't put it down', something you might say about a bestseller, *Beloved* was nonetheless hard to read: 'it took me about I think, it took me about six hours, in between cups of coffee and I actually re-read sections, because I found the language [difficult], some of it, some of the scenes in 124, I went back and read' (J). On occasions, though, such diligent re-reading was an insufficient way of controlling the narrative:

> this is anally retentive but I had to write down a couple of the names and where they fitted because I couldn't get, I couldn't get started into the book, I got confused a little bit with who was narrating who [...] who was the relationships between and it took me a while to actually do that, I write down or if there is a phrase or something, I usually, if I read, I often will have some paper with me and a pen (J).

In order to keep focused on the narrative, to maintain control, Julie creates a text of her own. Her belief that this technique is 'anally retentive' betrays, perhaps, a feeling that it is abnormal and should be unnecessary.

Despite the general agreement that *Beloved* was a 'hard book', defined variously at the level of form, style, and ideas, the readers were disinclined to critique it; the text was hard to read but this was not a source of censure. Madeleine told me that there was 'nothing really' that she disliked about the novel: 'it was a good book. Kept my attention, was well crafted in the terms of the way circumstances were described. I still remember it, the movie didn't do it justice' (M).[3] This type of response may have been influenced by the research methodology; readers may want to appear to have liked the text more than they really did. Also, considering the cultural prestige that Morrison has in some circles, readers may have felt pressured to concur. On the other hand, as I mentioned earlier, readers could have volunteered to be interviewed because the book had given them a pleasurable reading experience: 'I have to admit that if I had disliked it, I wouldn't have read it' (V). Zoe indicated how difficult she found the novel: 'maybe when I was, I don't know, maybe when I was reading it I disliked how difficult it was' (Z). Asked to define what she meant by 'difficult' she replied: 'I thought it was very difficult to read coz it was just kept chopping and changing [...] but then that difficulty is a challenge' (Z). Zoe is probably referring to the narrative structure of the novel, the complex 'chopping and changing' of narrators, chronologies and locations, but even this negative comment is equivocal; the difficulty of the novel makes it a challenge, and its capacity to challenge appears to be a good thing. This view was echoed by Winston: 'I found the ending puzzling, not that I dislike it ... I found it a challenging book and I, I you know I felt uncomfortable but that's what a good book should do, I think, you know?' (W). Here Winston suggests that the quality of a book is measured by the degree to which it disturbs the reader, a view that accords with numerous conservative and avant-garde cultural critics.

The novel's intricate form and baroque style are explained in a different way by Anthony. Although he also found it quite testing, he spoke about the novel's challenging nature in a more pragmatic way: 'at the beginning I was getting a bit frustrated ... I just wanted a sense of what it was all about, straight away, but that was revealed slowly, but then as I read I thought well, there was some benefit to that because you keep reading to find out' (A). Belinda, while not finding the novel 'too hard', still found it testing and tempting: 'because of its foreignness, in terms of its setting and also Toni Morrison's style, it kept me interested' (B). The book's complexities in this case are not so much a marker of value, or worth, as a technique or device for keeping the reader reading.

That the readers enjoyed a text which they considered difficult might be a measure of their confidence in their own cultural competency. The text issues a challenge or invitation which the readers feel capable of meeting and accepting. Moreover, if a text's 'resistance' to its readership may be regarded as a marker of value (Buckridge et al. 1995:25), then this stress on the difficulty of the novel could also be implicated in readers' self-representation. The readers may want to be seen as being capable of dealing with such a complex narrative.

Five ways of reading: making a novel mean

Despite the consensus that Beloved was complex novel, the readers offered a relatively narrow range of narrative interpretations. During the course of the interviews the readers articulated five ways in which they made the novel's narrative mean: biographically, autobiographically, generically, intertextually and historically. These ways of reading are best described as interpretative frames (Goffman 1975) or reading 'repertoires' which both enable and restrict reading (Fish 1980; Rose 2001). The use of these frames or repertoires constitutes the 'available knowledge', the mimetic capital, through which particular texts can be made meaningful (Hermes 1995:27). The knowledge of readers, the availability of frames of interpretation, places a limitation on the possible meanings of particular texts. Theoretically texts may well mean anything, but their meaning-in-use is always limited by the knowledge of the reader on the one hand, and structural properties of the text on the other. Furthermore, while the readers speak of their reading in terms of these five modalities, it is not safe to assume that this means that they actually read a book in that particular way because 'the argument that readers put forward do not necessarily reflect what they do with magazines [or books], but rather what they may wish to do with them or what they have fantasies of doing' (Hermes 1995:40). So when readers recount their reading experiences, they present not a record but a 'story of reading' (Martin 1986:171).[4] To interview readers is, ultimately, to hear someone represent their act of readership; the nature of people's representation of their cultural consumption then becomes the key question. It is more fruitful, therefore, to suggest that these five ways of reading *Beloved* are, in fact, ways in which the readers could *talk* about their reading of *Beloved*. These ways of speaking may have different degrees of correspondence to the fashion in which the novel was actually read; for the researcher, and for the reader, that original reading is always lost.

Reading books biographically

The first reading frame I would like to consider here is the biographical. I use the term 'biographical reading' not just to refer to readings that are negotiated in direct correspondence to the 'life of the author', but also to reading practices that use a conception, or knowledge, of an author as a triangulation point in the framing of meaning. The status of the author in the context of literary and cultural production has been subject to challenge and counter-challenge over recent decades. While the perceived status of the author may seem to impact only upon cultural production, defined in the traditional sense, it also has ramifications for the conceptualisation of the role of the reader as a cultural agent. From the perspective of liberal traditionalists the author is the origin of the singular meaning of the text (Barthes 1988:168). Reading under this formulation is restricted to the decoding, through the application of the correct interpretative techniques, of the author's meaning that is fully present in the text. Opposing this commonsense view of authorship and the intentional reading it demands (Porter Abbott 2002:95), other schools of criticism like new criticism, (post)structuralism and deconstruction, have all downplayed or even eradicated the role of the author as the source of meaning of a cultural work. As Malcolm Bradbury suggests, contemporary readers do so 'in two ages at once: the age of the author hyped and

promoted, studied and celebrated; the age of the author denied and elimi-
nated, desubjected and airbrushed from writing' (cited in Moran 2000:59).

Toni Morrison is a literary superstar so it might be expected that her status
would make biographical framings of the *Beloved* relatively common. However, awareness of the author among the readers was limited and it may be
the case that Morrison's celebrity status is far higher in the United States than
it is elsewhere. More generally, some readers knew little or nothing about
any of the authors they read, and seemed not to feel that their reading was
impoverished as a result. Their scant knowledge of Morrison could not alone
have formed a solid foundation for their interpretation of her novel; their
tendency to read biographically was therefore weak. Asked if he knew anything about *Beloved*, or its author, Anthony replied: 'no, not at all, nothing'
(A). Roz, similarly, knew nothing about Toni Morrison until a friend lent her
Beloved: 'nothing, never heard of her before in my life' (R). Furthermore,
reading the book does not seem to have sparked an interest in the author
either: 'no I haven't gone out of my way to find out who she is, I like her,
she's a good author but?' (R). Knowing about the author before reading a
book is then not important: 'no I don't think so' (R). In light of these comments it seems there is some validity to Ian Chambers's claim that everyday
culture is a field dominated by 'an aesthetics of distraction' (1986).

However, Roz and Anthony both undermine Chambers's too neat distinction between aesthetic and everyday cultures. Although it seems as if she
has little interest in anything beyond the novel itself, Roz makes the observation that not knowing about the author is a bonus because 'you can actually
find out about the author as you read along, if you're really getting into an
author and really love the books that they write' (R). Her lack of interest in
the author is then not as complete as it at first seems. Moreover, although
Anthony expressed no specific interest in the writer, he did feel a desire to
contextualise his reading: 'I'd like to find out more about this book ... whether
there's more to what's represented than what I perceived or, or not and if
I've missed something, that makes me want to [find out more]' (A). Roz's
and Anthony's reception of *Beloved* may not be 'appropriated through the
apparatus of [scholarly] contemplation' (Chambers 1986:12), but neither can
it be accurately described as distracted either. The extent to which Roz actually 'finds out' about the author as she reads, rather than constructs a fiction
of the author, is open to theoretical debate, but from the way she expresses
herself, an author certainly exists behind the text, an implied author that may
be known or (re)constructed through his or her fiction.

At the opposite pole on the continuum are the readers who follow a more
overtly humanist perspective; the author is perceived as a 'real' person who
contributes more or less directly to their reading practice. For someone like
Natasha, the author is a significant factor in reading:

> yes I do like to know about authors but they're not, you know, they're not
> more important, they don't change a book for me, I like to know who they are
> and what they're into [...] I do always read about the author if it has something
> to say and I like to see a picture of them (N).

Authors are important to Natasha, but not as the origin of a book's meaning.
Authors are significant, without a writer there would not be a text, but not to
the point where they overshadow or dictate her own interpretation. Another
reader, Belinda, described her relationship with a book's author as evolution-
ary: 'they're not important, but ... no they are not always important they
probably, they don't inspire me to read a book so much as evolve with my
interest in the book itself anyway' (B). In a similar way Vincent, who teaches
in the humanities at a metropolitan university and consequently has access
to many professional reading repertoires, suggests that authors still bring something positive to his experience of fiction:

> *In the author an important factor in your reading?*
> ... ultimately no, but I'm fascinated by authors, I like to know a bit about them.
> I actually think it does, it does affect the way one reads ... and I think with me,
> I don't know about other people, I need to locate people.
> *So it adds something?*
> it adds something, yeah (V).

Buckridge *et al.* showed that readers were disinclined to read a novel as
though it were an unmediated expression of the writer's personality (Buckridge
et al 1995:29). The ability to read novels in an expressive way requires presumably some knowledge of the author, a knowledge that not all readers
possess. But in the cases of Natasha, Belinda and Vincent outlined above,
the text is not thought to express the personality of the author as much as
the author functions as an augmentation of the text.

Of the readers who were able to speak about Morrison, their knowledge
was, when compared with that expected of a professional reader, highly
impressionistic. Belinda, despite a familiarity with the literary media and having worked in a bookshop, seemed to grasp few details about the author or
the novel. Asked about how she discovered the text, she replied:

> pretty much how I find out about most books which is the media, had talked
> about the author, I was aware that she was the winner of an award and I'd
> heard it was for this book, seen it in a bookshop saying you know award
> winning blah-dee-blah, and then I came across a friend who'd said they'd
> read it, yeah and they said it was brilliant and they'd lend it to me and before
> I knew it they shoved it in my hands and I had it and I had to go home and
> read it (B).

Later in the interview she added to her comments:

> I knew that she had written a couple of other books, one of her books had fairly recently come out, *Jazz* [*Paradise?*] [...] and that's probably where I saw she was an award-winning author, author of this other one *Beloved* and I may have read about the book on the web
>
> [...]
>
> actually, that's where I found out more about the book, the good old Oprah Winfrey blowing her own horn [laughs] yes I heard that what's it, Oprah Winfrey liked the book so much that she funded the movie and cast herself in the lead role (B).

Susan, who has a postgraduate qualification in English Literature and teaches English at a Sydney high school, also knew few details about Morrison when she read *Beloved*: 'I knew she was African-American, I knew that she was an English professor, I think that's all I knew about her, and that she was a writer' (S). Like Susan, Lana mentions Morrison's ethnicity, but also draws attention to her literary awards, her politics, and her association with Winfrey:

> I knew that, that Oprah was right behind her. I knew that she had won some prize or another, something to do with books, I knew she was black, I knew she was a bit radical and that was about it (L).

The connection between Morrison, *Beloved* and Winfrey is made frequently. Attitudes toward Winfrey are ambivalent to say the least. Lana removed the Oprah Book Club sticker from her copy of the novel: 'I did remove the [sticker], that's a symbolic gesture if ever you have one but no, I wonder if Oprah actually reads it sometimes' (L).[5] The removal of the book club imprimatur appears as a symbolic attempt to separate the television celebrity from the novel, an act of cultural decontamination, an attempt to re-establish a cultural hierarchy that the Book Club has, to some degree, blurred. It is this blurring of the lines of cultural distinction that led to Jonathan Franzen's refusal to allow his novel, *The Corrections*, to be chosen as a Book Club selection; Franzen was concerned that his position within the high-art tradition would be compromised if his novel were subject to such blatant commercialism (McCarthy 2002:8). At a later stage in the interview Lana gives voice to a more complex view of Winfrey's literary influence:

> I guess there are two different sides to Oprah, there's the Oprah that is self-help Oprah, for the masses, and then there is the Oprah that is diligently trying to indoctrinate people into the kinds of book she wants to read. She has a huge, huge influence on people, she's kind of like a social Bill Gates or something and that worries me, anyone with that amount of populist power worries me. But on the other side she is encouraging people to read books and people do buy it because of the sticker (L).

Here Lana splits the Oprah phenomenon in two. On one side there is 'self-help Oprah, for the masses', and on the other there is the Oprah who promotes reading. Significantly, in her formulation Lana appears to separate readers from 'the masses', and by association herself, and just as she separated *Beloved* from the Book Club sticker, so she separates the dangerous 'populist' Winfrey from her evangelistic literary shadow. The readers' creation of two Oprahs, self-helper and literary impresario, contrasts the view that these seemingly incommensurate roles are, in fact, perfectly compatible within the 'Change Your Life TV' paradigm because reading is both a tool of self-fashioning and a medium for understanding the individual's relationship with the social world (Parkin 2001:148).

The parallels notwithstanding, Lana was not the only reader who was troubled by the mixture of culture and commerce. When Roz tried to persuade a friend to read the novel she felt the need to explain to her that, 'even though it was on Oprah, it's still a good book' (R). Susan continues this pattern of ambivalence as she speaks of her feelings toward Oprah as a literary impresario:

> I think it's the ant's pants, I think she is the ant's pants for doing that day-time telly and look at all the results, all these people who are going out to buy books and want to, and want to know what Oprah thinks and what she's recommending.
>
> [...]
>
> I mean she's nauseating, [laughs] I don't, I don't know and she's obviously a multi-trillionaire as a result of being nauseating ... but I'm sure that she, I'm sure that she would feel quite strongly about, just being a black woman herself ... about promoting her own culture or something, I'd like to think that is wasn't totally an exercise in cynicism. Yes and even if it was ... would, would be a shame if it was, I'm sure it has, is, having positive results, for the book industry as well (S).

In these extended commentaries, both readers seem to be attempting to reconcile two different cultural ideologies; Winfrey is simultaneously the 'ant's pants' and 'nauseating'. There is a belief in the general benefit of reading—that the Book Club has encouraged more people to read more books is to be regarded as a good thing. But such literary evangelism that in another form might be a cause for celebration is compromised by its commercialism. Janice Peck argues that this conflict between culture and commerce is central to the Club's ideology which:

> simultaneously invokes and seems to undermine the binary logic that would categorically separate the 'queen' of the talk show (with its connotations of 'trash TV', passive consumption/viewing, vulgarity, low culture) from the champion of the literary (i.e. 'serious literature', active imagination/reading, refinement, high culture) (Peck 2000:231).

Crucially, this cultural conflict is embodied within individual cultural actors, rather than being crudely determined by a single social modality: class, gender or ethnicity. A conflict of cultural values within individual cultural actors has been a feature of other ethnographic research (Ang 1982). Some readers erect their own hierarchy of taste within a genre that may otherwise connote low and easy pleasures (Hermes 2000:225) or they may solve this conflict of values is by devaluing their books altogether (Frow *et al.* 1999). But for readers like Lana and Susan, the ideological divide is bridged in a different way because it is the context, rather than the text, that is regarded as embarrassing. By symbolically removing the text from the context, the book from the daytime television programme, the readers can save the novel from a threat of cultural contamination. That *Beloved* may be framed as an aesthetic object allows the readers to solve the dilemma, a solution not readily available to the viewers of soap-operas or the readers of Mills and Boon.

The fear of cultural contamination was not voiced by all the readers I interviewed. The high/low, or art/commerce, binary appears to be conspicuously absent from Julie's description of her introduction to *Beloved* via Oprah and the 'low-brow' medium of women's magazines:

> I read it 18 months ago, and whilst I knew that Toni Morrison had won the Nobel Prize, and thought she sounded like a really interesting writer to follow up on, I didn't do anything about it until I read, I read in a women's magazine about Oprah taking the, doing one of the roles in the film and how Morrison had been on set and actually hadn't liked her portrayal of the character and that made me go and read the book (J).

Although Julie knew that Morrison was a Nobel Laureate, this datum does not appear to have been as instrumental in her decision to read *Beloved* as does Morrison's tense relationship with the network television star; Winfrey is a more valuable sales engine than a Nobel Prize (McCarthy 2002:8).[6]

The connection between Morrison and Winfrey was not only made by the female readers: all four male interviewees too noted the relationship. In a situation not dissimilar to Julie's, Winston was quick to mention that he had first become aware of Morrison through her appearances on the hugely popular television show:

> *Did you know anything about Toni Morrison when you read Beloved?*
> no, I think I'd seen her on Oprah Winfrey's show when they were talking about whatever it was they were talking about, they were talking about her latest big book and they had a reading group there my impression of her was of a fiercely intelligent women, and you know, a fierce black woman, that was the thing, it was all tied up with race, so yes but beyond that it was a bit of a mystery, but certainly a strong impression (W).

Although the Winfrey connection does not appear to have provided the catalyst for Winston's reading of *Beloved*, as it did for Julie, it nonetheless informed Winston's reading. He told me that the novel:

> had a pretty big impact on me, I mean [...] because it was tied up with things like race and things like ... not just suffering and things not just like suffering but, but mass suffering, do you know and because I had, I think I had an idea of Morrison, and this is where biography is a factor, I had this idea of her being, I don't know if righteous is the right word, being you know angry and outspoken and you know, if she thought you weren't up to scratch she'd tell you sort of thing, there's a real sense of trepidation you know ...
>
> [...]
>
> there's so much loaded into it, race and that being such a sore kind of point, you have to be very careful what you say, so there is a real sense of trepidation, do I have the right to read this, do I have the right to you know, am I reading this the right way? (W).

Winston was not explicit as to why 'you have to be careful what you say' in this particular context. But there is a sense in which he may be implying that, as a white Anglo-Australian man, his speaking position precludes or circumscribes his response to the text; the novel is written by a black woman, about black experience and, therefore, this makes it difficult for him to speak his mind. Awareness of the author appears to have had a serious impact on Winston's approach to the book. Morrison's media image causes Winston to question his own reading practices to the point that he is afraid that he may be reading incorrectly: 'I feel like I can't criticise a great black American author' (W).

The Nobel Laureate is undoubtedly Winfrey's favourite writer, but none of the readers I interviewed would describe themselves as *aficionados* of Toni Morrison. Even though they told me that they had a high opinion of her novel, and some had read others besides *Beloved*, each would qualify as a 'social reader' under Becker's reader typology (1982). Madelaine, for instance, decided to read *Beloved* only by chance: 'I always hunt around the book section in Target,' because it has:

> a permanent 25 per cent off paperbacks. There is a lot of junk there, but now and again I find the odd jewel. I buy any authors I know and anything that looks as if it might be ok. I haven't got a dud yet (M).

Despite having read at least four of Morrison's novels (*Bluest Eye, Sula, The Song of Solomon* and *Beloved*) she claimed to know little about her, 'except she writes a good story' (M). This having been said, Madelaine then provided me with a biographical sketch of the writer about whom she claimed, only minutes before, to know nothing:

I imagine she is probably an activist there is that angry quality about her writing, or maybe that is just her particular type of fiction? Her characters have all suffered from and dealt with huge traumas, but there is redemption, I think she believes in redemption (M).

It is not possible to know if Madelaine is constructing an implied author from her reading of *Beloved*, or whether she actually does know more about Morrison than she realises, or is willingly, to relate. It is, however, insightful to compare her fragment of Morrison biography with comments she made elsewhere in the interview. When asked about what she liked in a book Madelaine stated clearly that although she enjoyed novels that dealt with serious topics, 'unrelenting blackness is not my style. I want a least a glimmer of redemption' (M). Moreover, when commenting on *Beloved* she described the novel as 'sort of redeeming really. It was sad in one sense and not in another' (M). Redemption is obviously a quality she likes in her books; it is a feature of the narrative of *Beloved* and an attribute of the implied author: 'I think she believes in redemption' (M). It is possible to make too much of this pattern, but I would suggest that Madelaine's representation of Morrison as a believer in redemption is analogous to Foucault's author/function (Foucault 1988). Madelaine constructs a biography of Morrison in a manner that supports, and legitimates, both her own understanding of the text and one of her book selection criteria.

Three of the readers knew of *Beloved* as the consequence of studying either it, or other Morrison novels, at school or university. It would perhaps be fair to expect that readers who encounter Morrison within an educational context would be well-placed to acquire a detailed knowledge of Morrison and her work. Zoe, for example, 'did *Beloved*' as part of a course on 'twentieth-century women writers', but by the time of the interview she had forgotten lots of things that she had once known about the book: 'yeah [laughs] sorry all I can remember, because it was so long ago, I can just remember, like yes the woman *Beloved* coming out of the lake and the killing of the babies, the thing where the riders come yes' (Z). The very specific and extensive repertoires needed to be a student-reader are often not maintained once a degree programme is completed.

Before studying the text formally Zoe knew nothing about either the book, or its author, but has since been inspired enough to read *Paradise* for pleasure. Conflating the biographical with the autobiographical frames, she explained that authors do have a significant role to play: 'yes I always read the bios [laughs] I can't help it, I think it is because I want to be a writer one day and I want to work out what they do' (Z). Knowledge of the author is important to her because:

it contextualises it, it adds something, like knowing that Morrison is a black African-American woman and knowing her whole like, yes, knowing that she studied literature at uni, and that she did literary criticism and stuff, yes it just adds something like ... you can see more I just I don't know, I see more what she wants to do with it, or what she might be wanting to do with it (Z).

Knowing about authors is not just important for *Beloved* however: '[f]or me it is important for all of it [books], but I don't know whether that's because I've studied English like, maybe with *Beloved* because it's such a difficult text it makes it easier to get a handle on it, sort of thing' (Z). Zoe here recognises the possible effects of institutionalised reading practices, albeit of a more traditional kind, on her own performance; indeed, she seems to finds it difficult to separate one from the other.

Like Zoe, Terri first encountered Toni Morrison's writing as part of a university course: she 'had' to read *Jazz*. As a result, when it came to reading *Beloved* she 'knew what was coming' (T), and like Zoe, she sees value in knowing something about authors in general and Morrison in particular:

I guess well, for example with Toni Morrison it, it means something to me that she is African-American and that's what she is writing about.
What does that do to the book?
Well it gives it some authenticity for me ...
Even though she didn't experience the things she writes about, how does it make it authentic?
I think one of the really lovely things about that book is the way she produces speech and it has a real rhythm to it and she's, she's catching the way certain people speak and, and I think that is because she's sort of inside that herself (T).

Terri's reading of *Beloved* is enhanced by the perceived authenticity of Morrison's speaking position. Authenticity in this instance does not derive from the direct personal experience of the author, but from her membership of a particular ethnic or racial group. Consequently, Morrison is able to use writing to reconstruct a historical idiom which is, itself, used as a marker of authenticity. Subscribing to an expressive realism, the normative understanding that a creative form expresses an anterior reality (Belsey 1980:13), Terri's awareness of the ethnicity of the writer makes the narrative more affective. This humanist belief in the presence of the author in the text is often represented as an outdated and unequivocally conservative belief within the academy, one that should be rejected. But for Terri, the 'presence' of a black, female author in a novel that deals with the effects of slavery in nineteenth-century America makes the novel more convincing and more believable in its social critique. The liberal humanist approach to authorship that had once sought to universalise or generalise meanings is re-deployed to authenticate more specific, in this instance African-American, cultural experiences. Race, class, gender and ethnicity, all once elided by appeals to a universal reading and writing subject, have now become markers of authenticity itself (Weedon 1997:157).

Overall, Morrison does seem to have played some role in the majority of readers' relationships with *Beloved*. In this sense their reading practice supports Dugald Williamson's claim that, despite rumours to the contrary, 'the author is a key component with various practices of writing, publishing, distributing, classifying, interpreting and valorising texts' (Williamson 1989:2).

Reading books autobiographically

Unlike biographical reading, which requires at least some cognisance of the author, autobiographical reading—the framing of a text within the experiences of a particular reader—requires little cultural capital. Autobiographical repertoires generally lack favour within many institutional contexts. Culture warrior Alan Bloom is critical of this autobiographical reading as a crude and aberrant method of framing a text that the education system should aim to eradicate (Bloom 1984:63). Despite this illegitimate status, an autobiographical frame does allow people with minimal formal training to make sense of what they read (Becker 1982:46). The experiences and memories of the reader are a readily available resource when other more legitimate, specialised or authoritative means of framing are not. As a repertoire of 'last resort', autobiographical reading should not to be confused with a 'universal' or 'natural' reading of a text because each reader's own autobiographical repertoire is itself the product of a personal, and therefore, social history.[7]

In an autobiographical fashion, the readers make connections between the Morrison's novel and certain elements of their own life experiences. In the following excerpt, Zoe relates her reading of the novel to her position as a medical student:

> I just, I just love the way she can make something so horrible beautiful [laughs] like infanticide, to take infanticide and make it so beautiful like the book actually does yeah, I'm doing med [medicine] I get really overcome by the public health aspect, especially when I'm reading reports, all the time about infant mortality and stuff, whereas to read a novel that just makes it beautiful [...] I like the way she'll take an issue as complex as that and bring it out (Z).

This autobiographical reading takes the form of an intersection between the life narrative of the reader and a single aspect of the novel, but reading in the autobiographical mode is manifest itself in other ways. A different use of the autobiographical frame is evident in Anthony's discussion of the physical and emotional hardships represented in the novel:

> I just, even though they were much more harsh experiences those people went through, I identified in some way, to some amounts of things in my own

life like I've experienced, so I sort of related a little even though these were far more traumatic (A).

Importantly, such an autobiographical reading is not just an empirical search for an exact correspondence between novel and life narratives. Identification is more than just a 'that's me' (Brown 1996:63) reading strategy because it 'implies not just a one-to-one correspondence' between reader and text, but a broader, multifarious association (Morley and Silverstone 1990:47). This creative identification of readers is well demonstrated by Zoe:

> I guess I like to relate to a book, like well, I like to sometimes, I like to yes read something that relates to an experience I've had, but not necessarily in the way I've had it, like often in a really different way, but that I can still understand (Z).

Similarly, Anthony's autobiographical reading of *Beloved* is not one of 'one-to-one correspondence', but a reading made through creative appropriation. These acts of cultural and symbolic appropriation include the 'locking and mooring of the "objective possibilities" of selected items,' in this case certain aspects of the narrative, 'to the sensibilities and interests, hopes and fears of their users' (Willis 1990:74). Anthony takes Morrison's fictional world, distant in both time and place from his own real-life experiences, and tethers it to his own sensibilities.

One method that a reader might employ to creatively appropriate a narrative is empathy. An empathetic approach to identification is clearly articulated in this reader's guide to Morrison's novels:

> The most a novel can hope to achieve is to render its characters so convincingly that we put some part of ourselves in their place, feel some of what they feel. If you were a slave, what would they do to your body, mind, spirit, soul, memory? What would they do to your parents, friends, children? What would it cost you to survive that or to stand by and watch it? (David 2000:127)

Anthony, clearly, did not read the novel in this fashion. Rather than closing the gap between reader and character, as an empathetic reading requires, Anthony maintains his distance and as result, reads not with empathy but affinity, an affinity that is produced in the dialectic between his reality and Morrison's representation, in the tension between (dis)similar life experiences and the knowledge provided by the narrative. Significantly, Morrison speaks of the importance of such 'similes of identification' (Miall 2006:306) in her own reading; as a child she was particularly fond of Dostoevsky, Tolstoy and Austen: even though 'those books were not written for a little black girl in Lorain, Ohio, but they were so magnificently done that I got them anyway—they spoke directly to me out of their own specificity' (cited in David 2000:9).

As well as providing isolated moments of identification, autobiographical frames of interpretation may also contribute to a reader's totalising interpretation of a narrative. Julie, for example, speaks of the novel's depiction of mundane events and banal issues that nonetheless have great significance. Speaking of the house in and around which much of *Beloved*'s narrative is situated, Julie told me that, 'it's scary but then again you can relate to it, and I think what the book did for me, it put words to a lot of things that, that are sort of silent subjects' (J). When asked to elaborate she replied:

> Well, I think family madness is one of them [laughs] and I mean even just having, you know, a kind of crazy auntie, or an alcoholic father or, I mean nothing would be as bad as that but there are elements in 124 that overflow into one's own life (J).

Julie's reading, in this aspect at least, appears to have taken a distinctly autobiographical hue, the book 'overflow[s] into one's life', the barriers between the real and fictive worlds become permeable. To this end, Julie uses the novel to meditate upon her relationship with her own mother: 'I thought I envied Beloved being named Beloved, I though what a beautiful, beautiful name and how I would love my mother to have loved me so much, she would've called me Beloved and not just [Julie]' (J).

Such an autobiographical repertoire surfaces repeatedly throughout her interview. In another example, Julie uses her life story to legitimate her comments about the novel. Speaking of the novel's representation of the hardships of rural life, Julie said with a sense of dismay: 'these wonderful young men reduced to ... buggering cattle, the suppression' (J). Asked if she found the depictions of bestiality confronting she replied 'no' because 'I come from the farm' (J). In this instance, her experiences of growing up in rural Australia—generalised as 'the farm'—underpin her response to the text, experiences that operate as an authenticity affect, legitimising her interpretations.

Reading books generically

As well as biographical and autographical frameworks, the readers also read within a third frame: genre. Not simply reading against a fixed or objective pattern, reading generically requires the use of experiences and knowledge gained from encounters with other similar books (Cobley 2001:214). If I had concentrated on detective or romance fiction, then genre would likely have been a primary consideration. However, the expectation that the readers would use a generic repertoire to read a novel like *Beloved* is low because it is a book that comes wrapped a multitude of aesthetic codes. Indeed, capital 'L' literature's privileged position is reliant on its status as 'not-genre-fiction'

(Batsleer 1997:21-22). While it would be wrong to overstress the frequency with which readers used a generic repertoire, the fact that a few readers did frame *Beloved* in this way is noteworthy.

Where the generic repertoire did feature, it was present in two forms. First, readers told me that *Beloved* was an example of magic-realism. Significantly, Morrison has tried to avoid such a categorisation and in an interview she explained that: 'you've got to call [*Beloved*] something. Just as long as they don't call me a magic realist' (cited in Gilroy 1993:181). Unperturbed by the Nobel Laureate's injunction, Winston told me that he was uncertain 'how to make sense of [*Beloved*] because it is this magic-realist kind of thing' (W), and Vincent too notes the magic-realist aspects of the text:

> I think there are some parallels with, some parallels with magic-realist writers just because kind of those super-real elements, I have to admit I'm getting kind of tired of magic-realism (V).

Belinda enjoys the novel in its realist moments, but the enjoyment is broken when the realism becomes fantastic. For her, the most memorable section of the novel was the opening few chapters:

> I think I enjoyed the first part of the book before the main character arrives at, is it Sweet Home?
>
> [...]
>
> *Before Beloved arrives?*
> Yes, before Beloved arrives?
> *Where Paul D comes and they go to the fair?*
> yes, yes and I think that's because ... it's quite a historical, possibility in because telling of what may, what it may have been like in that era without any of the sort of fantasy, spiritual, ghosts and things like that coming in to it. (B).

These supernatural elements meant that she 'couldn't engage with the characters or relate to their experience' (B). As a result of such genre-shifting, even the representations of infanticide failed to make an impression:

> No, I couldn't no, no [relate to the book] it went very closely consistently to, the side of not being able to believe it but because of that blend of fantasy, or things I don't consider to be real, meant that I couldn't go along believing them or pushed to that length and understand that, that was part of the book (B).

This reader finds it impossible to assimilate the two, as she sees it, divergent and contradictory aspects of the book. Belinda does not use the term magic-realism, unlike Winston and Vincent, even though her description of the novel would appear to come close to the conventions of the genre.[8] Without an awareness of the generic framework which would have allowed her see the narrative as whole, its realistic and fantastic elements were simply confusing, and this confusion detracted from Belinda's overall reading pleasure. In retrospect I am surprised that, at no stage, did I ask the readers to define what they meant by magic-realism. This type of retrospective self-questioning is a characteristic of ethnographic or interview-based research: to an extent the significance of a particular comment, or insight, comes at the point of analysis rather than enunciation (Wolcott 1995:86). But in this case, the reason for not pursuing my informants' definitions of the genre was determined by an intersection of my and my readers' textual practice; because we 'knew' what we meant by the term 'magic-realism', questions of definition did not arise.

The second fictional genre deployed by the readers is that of the gothic. More accurately, the gothic genre was used specifically by just a single reader, and tangentially by others. To Roz, the gothic aspects of Morrison's novel were appealing: 'I like, liked the gothicness of it' (R). Later she added: 'American gothic ... kind of the whole scary baby thing [that] was very well done in that it wasn't the whole poltergeist kind of head swivelling which is very unsubtle' (R). Roz's ability to read *Beloved* as a gothic novel is predicated on her detailed knowledge of that genre. It is not surprising that gothic novels are among her preferred types of books: Clive Barker, Anne Rice, Angela Carter and Christopher Fowler are named as favourite writers.

Reading books intertextually

Generic reading is at least partially intertextual reading, which is the fourth way in which the readers frame their encounters with *Beloved*. The term intertextuality possesses numerous meanings. At one end of a broad spectrum of usage, intertextuality refers to 'a free floating intersubjective body of knowledge', at the other, 'the explicit presence of other texts within a given work by focusing on the processes of citation, reference, etc.' (Collins 1989:44). I use the term here to refer to a reader's ability to locate one book by reference to another. This 'intertextual arena' (Collins 1989:43) provides an alternative to reading within a generic frame (Buckridge *et al.* 1995:28) and there seems to be a logical assumption that reading intertextually may be easier than reading generically. In the readers' textual economy of *Beloved*, however, the promise of the intertextual frame was never fully realised.

Amongst the readers I interviewed providing a ready intertext for *Beloved* proved a very difficult task. When asked for a comparable text Anthony replied: 'Like this one? no, none at all' (A). Although readers had difficulty in grasping ready analogues for *Beloved* they made some comparisons. The novel was variously compared with the book and television series of Alex Hayley's *Roots* (B), the film of Alice Walker's *The Color Purple* (F), and Irene Jacobs's novel *Incidents in the Life of a Slave Girl* (L). One reader even said that *Beloved* was reminiscent of *Gone with the Wind* (J). When they were able the readers framed the novel within fictional representations, across a range of forms, of African-American social history. A solitary reader, however, broke this frame and made the comparison between Morrison's novel and the work of Australian Aboriginal playwright and poet Jack Davis who describes 'the level of poverty' but not with 'that same power and tension' (J). This Australian reader draws an intertextual connection that would likely not be made by a reader elsewhere. Nonetheless, it is also far too simplistic to suggest that simply because *Beloved* is read in Australia it will be read in this way; Julie was the only reader to make any connection at all between the social history of African-Americans and that of indigenous Australians.

The complex web of intertextual relationships in which the text may be implicated is demonstrated by Frances:

> when I got the book it was a copy that had 'now a motion picture' or something, and it said it had Oprah Winfrey in it and I thought it might be good. I don't know it sounds a bit corny but she [Oprah] seems to choose rather intense sort of things to be in, I liked *The Color Purple* and she was in that, and I think she did a pretty good job of it. I just thought I like to see it [*Beloved*] too (F).

This reader seems to make a positive connection, in relation to the film, between Oprah Winfrey and Morrison's novel. The novel is connected by the reader, via promotional information printed on its cover, to Winfrey's role in the film adaptation of Alice Walker's *The Color Purple*. This intertextual weave forms, across media, the basis of certain deductions about the narrative: *The Color Purple* is intense, *Beloved* is likely to be also. These intertextual relationships indicate the media literacy of this particular reader and may also reveal the complex 'synergy' between different cultural forms across the mediascape. This synergy is driven by certain relations of production in which large media conglomerates have a commercial interest in a diverse range of media products: 'there is clearly great potential for synergy in the area of book publicity, which involves selling books through other mass media [magazines, newspapers, television, radio, film] often owned by the same parent company' (Moran 2000:39). Intertextual relationships like those articulated by the readers may then reveal the occult influences and alliances of diffuse media empires.

Others readers were able to frame *Beloved* intertextually, albeit within less complex relationships. A few readers placed the book in relation to what they considered to be similar novels and writers:

> *The Bone People* by Kerrie Hulme which was a novel I read, which really impressed me and had the same sort of magic-realism and was about the same kind of things, race and dispossession and stuff (W).

> I mean the other I would compare it to is Margaret Atwood ... (W).

so I guess the book does stick out in my memory I think, I mean it's the same era as *The Bone People* (V).

The Grass Dancer, Susan Power is one that comes to mind, sort of the same feel about it, different stories of course (M).

The readers make a connection between Morrison's novel and other texts on the basis of genre, 'feel', subject matter and author. There are numerous possible points of contiguity between *Beloved*, *The Bone People* and *The Grass Dance*. Toni Morrison (African-American), Susan Power (Native American) and Kerri Hulme (Pakeha/Maori) may all be described as 'ethnic' women writers; the novels combine real and fantastic elements; and the narratives all deal with the experience of colonised peoples and their communities. Nevertheless, much like the generic frame, overt intertextual considerations of *Beloved* did not generate a great deal of enthusiasm on the readers' behalf.

Reading books historically

Beloved is certainly regarded as a work of fiction by the readers. This is clearly indicated by the readers' choices of intertexts: all are fictional forms regardless of medium. Fiction though it may be, the readers spoke of how their readings of the novel furnished them with what they believe to be specific sociological and historical knowledge. Surprisingly, perhaps, the national report *Books Alive* concluded that, in terms of attitudes toward reading, 'only one statement generated broad agreement across all demographic groups: reading is good because you learn things' (*Books Alive* 2001:63).[9] That readers accrue knowledge from reading novels is a counterbalance to two dominant beliefs about fiction-reading. First, everyday fiction-reading is not just about escapism, a use of books long the topic of scholarly opprobrium (Nussbaum 1995). Second, the pleasures of fiction-reading are thought to be linked to the imagination not information (Buckridge *et al.* 1995:11). This information/imagination binary in text-reader relations is articulated here, in the context of television viewing, by John Corner:

> the characteristic properties of text-viewer relations in most non-fiction television are primarily to do with kinds of knowledge, usually regulated and framed by direct address speech .... The characteristic properties of text-viewer relations in fictional televisions are primarily to do with imaginative pleasure, particularly the pleasures of dramatic circumstance and of character (cited in Barker 1997:22, original emphasis).

This distinction between fiction and non-fiction was in no way so clearly defined by the readers. Like Hermes' detective fiction readers for whom 'sociocultural, anthropological and historical background knowledge' were as much part of the genre's appeal as 'suspense' (2000:224), my informants regarded fiction in general as a conduit for knowledge and, in the case of *Beloved*, historical knowledge in particular. Indeed, the readers were at their most animated when speaking of *Beloved* and history. The richness of this repertoire could be explained by both the wide circulation of representations of post-civil war American society and, more generally, a tendency for readers to regard all narratives set in a recognisable past as historical.

Readers' assertions that novels are a source of knowledge might be a justification for reading fiction in a utilitarian world or, alternatively, for readers of genre fiction especially, a means to legitimate an illegitimate fictional form. But there seems to be no reason why gaining of knowledge may not form part of the pleasure of fiction-reading (Eco 1992:147), other than to perhaps enforce a rather schematic knowledge/pleasure dichotomy. Some years ago Richard Hoggart made a case for fiction as a neglected source of knowledge: he asks rhetorically, is literature not 'really a form of knowledge?' (Hoggart 1970:21). Moreover, George Watson later contended that a 'novel is a fund of knowledge as well as a literary form' (Watson 1979:3).

The relationships between literature, history, and knowledge have been well documented by critics working within a broad range of ideological and theoretical traditions (Watt 1963; Colebrook 1997). In his seminal *The Rise of the Novel* (1963), Ian Watt argues that the novel form made possible the literary representation of the 'modern sense of time' and its appearance coincided with 'a more objective study of history and therefore of a deeper sense of the difference between the past and the present' (Watt 1963:24). Western Marxism has argued that literature offers a knowledge of reality, which includes historical knowledge (Jefferson and Robey 1992:172), and early humanist proponents of the novel attempted to legitimate the form by claiming, on its behalf, 'a new dignity as history' (Watson 1978:99). The idea that fiction provides knowledge both pre- and post-dates the rigid distinction between documentary and imaginative writing that has been dominant since the nineteenth century. A belief in the absolute distinction between fictional and non-fictional writing is based on an unsophisticated formulation of the 'real world' and an equally crude separation of that world 'from the observation and imagination' of people (Williams 1971:41).

The ability of the readers to glean historical knowledge from *Beloved* is demonstrated here by Roz:

> I liked finding out about all the slavery stuff which I didn't, never knew before, I mean I knew slavery was bad obviously, everyone does, and you know basic things but she actually brought it a lot more to life (R).

Roz speaks of *Beloved* as if it were a record of historical fact: the novel helps her 'find out' about slavery, to uncover a hidden past. The narrative supplements her rudimentary understanding of the operation and effects of slavery, in a way comparable to a historical non-fiction. One method of articulating history to the novel is expressed by Terri:

> I guess I was also informed reading that book because I just finished reading a lot of African-American history and that really helped me too, because I wouldn't have known a lot of the circumstances were not stated, they were sort of referred to ... (T)

In the context of her reading of *Beloved*, historical texts give Terri a clearer understanding of Morrison's diegetic world. Terri's view of the relationship between the novel and history represents a common means of relating the two orders of discourse. Such an approach seems to privilege the novel, but could also be said to attribute an explanatory power to history (Bennett 1988:46). The shift of genre, and with it the change in epistemic privilege, seems not to be a concern for Terri's textual ecumenism. In contrast, the following reader grapples with the ontological boundaries that appear, unsatisfactorily though they seem, to separate historical fact from historical fiction:

> the part where the guy [Paul D] is in the prison in the South, you know in those boxes under the ground, and they are all chained up, that has so much detail that that I think that must be real, but then I think it's mixed in with all the supernatural elements, so ... (W).

Despite Winston's articulation of the differences between history and fiction he still speaks of the narrative as if it were a 'true' account of past events. Regardless of his uncertainty, Morrison's narrative has altered his perception of slavery:

> and I guess I also never realised that ... that that sort of thing happened, you know I thought slavery, at the time I thought plantations, whips and you know just ... I didn't realise yes ... it was very horrible, it was a horrifying book (W).

That novels may offer their readers a form of historical knowledge is a hypothesis that would probably be supported by the *Beloved* readers I spoke to. From a more theoretical perspective, however, the relationship between fiction and history can be thought of differently; the novel has a 'supplementary' relationship with history. More than just providing readers with historical narratives, the novel acts simultaneously as the other of historical fact and as a place from which the fictionality of history and its limits as an account of real events are exposed (Fleischman 1978:15). To a greater extent than any fictional form, the novel 'forces the fiction-history problematic' on its readership (Mayer 1997:15).

Although she is certainly not consciously deconstructing history in the academic sense of the term, Julie certainly goes beyond articulating a simple equivalence between historical novels and history by suggesting that Morrison actually writes better 'history' than historians:

> her story says more to me about the condition of black and white people in that time than probably any historian might tell me in a history book.
> *Why do you think that is?*
> because I'm engaged with the story, you know, I'm not, I'm not a spectator [...] I'm a participant.
> [...]
> I would tend to put the history book down and think, you know, something I didn't think about or, but it doesn't make me think, it doesn't engage me in the same way that a novel does. And I think that, that's the power in the storytelling (J).

Reading *Beloved* as history is, for Julie, phenomenologically different from reading historical non-fiction; fiction affords a higher degree of personal involvement. This sentiment is also expressed by Roz. She told me that she knew 'nothing' or 'very little' about 'slavery and American history', and that 'even though, you know, it's not something I'd probably choose to read if I had a choice, like I wouldn't go out of my way to read about slavery and stuff', she still found the novel very enjoyable. I asked her if 'there is a difference between reading a history book about slavery and reading a novel about slavery.'

> yeah for sure, what's it, like I was saying, 10,000 people died, that's just a number, but if you focus on one person, if one person dies in a novel ... that hits you a lot harder that 10,000 people I think, I just phrased that really badly [laughs] the emotional element basically, history doesn't believe in emotion.
> *But novels do?*
> Yes and actually brings it a lot more to life (R).

In lauding the form's ability to personalise historical events, Julie's and Roz's comments echo Watt's argument that one of the novel's major attributes has been its ability to individualise larger historical processes by locating characters in a specific place and time (Watt 1963:22). Near the close of the interview, true to the contradictory nature of ethnographic research, Julie reveals that:

> I don't know much about slavery so I haven't, I can't compare any kind of historical documents or books about slavery, and that affected me, but I'm sure that they wouldn't in the way, in the way *Beloved* did (J).

So her comparison between *Beloved*, as a historical novel, and conventional historical accounts is not based on any actual reading of American or African-American histories. Her opinion that *Beloved* is better than a historical non-fiction text is an instance of a generally held belief, a vernacular 'theory of the novel' even, rather than an isolated or specific instance.

In his discussion of the appeal of fiction and its relationship with 'reality', Avrom Fleischmann contends that: '[w]hatever it is that fiction, among other literary forms, says, it is presumably something that non-literary writing doesn't say, fully, exclusively, or satisfactorily' (Fleischman 1978:13). In Julie and Roz's case, a novel like *Beloved* seems to offer a sense of personal participation, an affective realism that they cannot derive from historical non-fiction. Moreover, Roz's historical framing of the text appears to have an ethical or moral dimension:

> I was surprised at the, my response to it actually, when she's talking about children being sold off like cattle, people being bred [that] really offended me and really I thought that was incredibly disgusting, I couldn't believe that anybody could actually think like that, I realised that they did obviously ... yes I was surprised, I was glad of my response, I thought, yes, enlightened girl (R).

That Roz describes herself as an 'enlightened girl' is revealing because such an interpretation of her reading dovetails with Morrison's own view of the purpose of her writing. Morrison argues that one of the 'very strong functions' of a novel is that it should 'work' as well as be 'beautiful and powerful'. Accordingly, a novel must function beyond the aesthetic domain, it 'should have something in it that enlightens; something in it that opens the door and points the way' (Morrison 1990:328). Novels may test readers' ethical capacity, and in so doing the privations and struggles of others may be understood (Chabot Davis 2004:413). There is a strong sense in which Roz has attributed to the text just this sort of ethical effect. David Carter has made the point that such ethical reflection is a major attraction of book reading in the post-print age. Book readers he suggests—especially those reading with book-clubs or reading groups—engage in a process of linking the self with history and politics, the private with the public, '*through reading*' (Carter 2001:4, original emphasis).

Of all the readers who framed *Beloved* historically, Julie seemed the keenest to speak of the novel in this historical manner. Her fondness for the historical repertoire was enhanced by a visit to America soon after first reading Morrison's book. Just as readers use experience to mediate the text, as in Anthony's affinity with the extreme hardships portrayed in the novel discussed earlier, so this process may work in reverse; texts mediate our everyday experiences by providing interpretative frames through which those encounters may be partially codified. In an attempt to explain the novel, Julie uses the narrative to interpret New York City's ethnoscape:

> it's too glib to say you know it's [*Beloved*] about inequality or it's about you know the reality of black American life, because to me it [*Beloved*] resonated, and still does because not long after that I went to New York and I was living in

Harlem and actually saw or witnessed a slightly better way of life, but still
having not moved very far ...

[...]

I think you see who has the, the low level jobs in a place like New York you
certainly know, I never saw white people driving buses, cleaning apartments,
working as sort of concierges, selling bananas on the corner of you know
Broadway and 25th, it was either Afro-Americans, Indians, or Latinos (J).

In her commentary, which could be a form of informal ethnography itself,
Julie combines the knowledge gained from reading *Beloved* with the experiences garnered, 'witnessed', while visiting America. In fact, it is possible to
suggest that her experiences in New York actually support her reading of the
novel. When she claims that African Americans are currently living 'a slightly
better life, but still having not moved very far', she probably means 'very far'
from the living conditions represented in Morrison's book; again there is a
continuity, rather than a distinction, between the diegetic and extra-diegetic
worlds. As Steven Connor speculates, 'it may be that experience is always, if
not actually determined, then at least interpreted in advance by the various
structures of understanding and interpretation' (Connor 1997:3) to which
texts contribute. In this instance, Julie relates a situation in which her 'first-
hand' experiences and 'second-hand' knowledge work together. This having
been said, it is always possible for experience and knowledge to clash, sometimes violently, as one is never entirely reducible to the other.

In their willing conflation of history and fiction, the readers appear to
contradict Harold Bloom's predictably negative claim that '[h]istory writing
and narrative fiction have come apart, and our sensibilities seem no longer to
accommodate them one to another' (Bloom 1994:21). Indeed, it is almost
the case that my readers chose not to differentiate between them; in their
minds they are linked. From a different critical perspective, the weave of
historical 'fact' with historical 'fiction' that seems to be part of the readers'
historical repertoire could be read as symptomatic of the shallowness of a
postmodern culture. Under such cultural conditions, the modernist-
postmodernist Frederic Jameson asserts that 'the historical novel can no longer
set out to represent the historical past; it can only "represent" our ideas and
stereotypes about that past (which thereby at once becomes "pop history")'
(Jameson 1991:25). Against this now rather tired 'end of history' debate,
Raphael Samuel makes the case that the expansion of the mass media has
probably expanded, rather than reduced, 'historical culture' (Samuel 1994:25).
Likewise, Alejandro Bayer is also critical of the orthodox view that contemporary western societies are 'amnesiac cultures' because, to the contrary,
'we are living through a moment characterized by an unprecedented presence of history and memory in the cultural sphere' (Bayer 2001:492). Rather
than exemplifying the collapse of the social into the aesthetic, I feel that the

readers' historical reading of *Beloved* actually contests Jameson's totalising claims. The readers use Morrison's novel to expand or even criticise their accepted understanding of slavery: 'I also never realised that that sort of thing happened' (W); 'I liked finding out about all the slavery stuff which I didn't, never knew before' (R). I am certainly not arguing that *Beloved* gives the readers access to a 'real' experience of slavery outside representation, but the novel has made some of them question their own conventional knowledge and understanding, or lack thereof. As Belinda told me, 'the subject matter was something that I had not been exposed to at all before either, the black slave story from the perspective of a black American and being an historical account made it really quite unique' (B). It is not possible to use such a small group of readers to refute completely Jameson's apocalyptic vision, but Winston, Roz, Julie, Belinda and Terri's historical readings should act as a reminder that actual cultural practices always, to some degree, resist such grand theoretical visions.

Conclusion

Although the novel challenged the readers' expectations and their reading competency, all readers offered a positive opinion of Morrison's text. The way in which they articulated their feelings and narrative interpretations seems to make an absolute distinction between everyday and professional textual practice difficult. The interpretative frames deployed by the readers are not completely different from those that could operate within educational contexts. While educational institutions are unlikely to encourage students to read *Beloved* autobiographically, they could certainly position the text as a historical, gothic or magic-realist novel, as a text on a black women's writing course or even as part of an author study. The presence of such 'academic' repertoires within the textual economy of everyday reading seems to support David Carter's assertion that within the domain of the textual economy, at least, attempts to simply divide the reading population into academic and public—or even '"academic *versus* public"—seriously misrepresents the diversity and cross-over of reading cultures' (Carter 2001:4, original emphasis). This overlap between academic and everyday framing of the novel could be seen as a product of the high level and type of education of the interviewees. Frames of reading acquired during secondary and tertiary education have persisted into a general reading practice. Yet despite this educational influence the amount of available knowledge within each frame was not extensive. Readers' framings lacked the plenitude of details and discourses available to the professional reader. The operation of a textual economy of reading is finally an argument for the retention of textual analysis. Whereas text-based studies are largely ineffective in locating the spatial and social economies of everyday reading, they may be very effective in positing possible ways in which texts *may* be framed by readers. However, only attention to the readers' performance of the text can show which frames are actualised in everyday living.

Notes

1. See Morrison's edited collection *Race-ing, Justice, Engendering Power: Essays on Anita Hill, Clarence Thomas, and the Construction of Social Reality* (1993).
2. Morrison co-edited and wrote the introduction to *Birth of a Nationhood: Gaze, Script, and Spectacle in the O.J. Simpson Case* (1997).
3. In general, very few of the readers had seen the film adaptation, and those that had were not impressed.
4. Virginia Nightingale (1996), notes the narrative dimension of such research: 'viewers translate their viewing experience into the sorts of stories they believe the researchers will find interesting' (Nightingale 1996:x).
5. This is an interesting point. *Beloved* has never been an official Book Club choice, so the appearance of a sticker denoting such a selection would appear to be an astute, if disingenuous, marketing strategy.
6. According to P. David Marshall the daily audience for 'The Oprah Winfrey Show' was huge in the 1990s: 15 million American viewers, 113 million viewers worldwide (Marshall 1994:132).
7. See Christian (1993) for a discussion of race and the autobiographical framing of *Beloved*.
8. Magic-realist 'writers interweave, in an ever shifting pattern, a sharply etched *realism* in representing ordinary events and descriptive details together with fantastic and dreamlike elements, as well as with materials derived from myths and fairy tales' (Abrams 1999:195-96).
9. While only 13 per cent read to 'escape', 36 per cent of interviewees said they read to gain knowledge (*Books Alive* 2001:57).

Coda – 'Doing Things with Books': Listening to Everyday Readers

It is a fallacy to assume that the swarming, unpredictable and problematic mess in which human beings live can be understood on the basis of what books—texts—say; to apply what one learns out of a book literally to reality is to risk folly or ruin.

Edward Said, Orientalism

It was certainly an error to suppose that values or art-works could be adequately studied without reference to the particular society within which they were expressed.

Raymond Williams, The Long Revolution [end]

In this book I have discussed at length the complexity of a small group of readers' everyday book culture. For these educated, city-dwelling readers, novel-reading continues to appeal despite the proliferation of new media. Book-reading remains attractive, at least in part, because it is a highly adaptable cultural activity. Unlike other cultural practices that require large amounts of specific equipment, extensive preparation, a dedicated space, or even other participants, everyday reading is more immediately available. As one reader told me 'reading is very portable, all you need is words and light' (M). Of course, you do actually need a lot more than just 'words and light' to be able to read but, generally, the reader's point is well made. From the readers' stories, it seems clear that as well as its flexibility, book-reading is also appealing because it is a versatile cultural activity. Commentators sometimes suggest that books and reading are doomed because information can be found quicker and easier through the internet: 'when we are hungry we tend to reach for the most convenient fare' (Young 2007:65). Such an assertion is correct insofar as books can be considered databases. To assume that reading is only about accruing information demonstrates an attenuated understanding of the uses to which readers put their books.

Clearly, the readers I interviewed use books in many different ways: books provide materials for living. Books are used as a form of education, for information and ideas certainly, but they are also used to cope with the stress of commuting, for physical and psychological comfort, to pass the time, as a panacea for loneliness and as a means of manufacturing solitude. Books are a means to create and maintain personal relationships, to provide vicarious experiences, to transform the space in which they read, and to gain the pleasure that is derived from both a writer's skill in fabricating a compelling narrative and in anticipation of 'what comes next'. Importantly, these divergent uses can manifest themselves simultaneously: a single reading per-formance produces a number of meanings, uses and pleasures. So, to the frequently asked question, 'what do readers do with their books', this book offers a sophisticated and richly rendered answer.

One reader even told me that reading novels had helped him overcome his alcoholism which had developed during his years in the fishing industry in north Queensland. During long periods out at sea, sometimes as long as a week or ten days, book-reading presented him with an alternative to watch-ing videos and drinking heavily with his ship-mates. Rather than mix with the others, he would lock himself in his cabin with an assortment of the longest novels he could find by authors like Stephen King and George Eliot, Marcel Proust and Eric van Lustbader, often purchased simply because they were good value for money (A). Reading *The Stand* and *Middlemarch* allowed him to cope with his addiction to alcohol, itself precipitated by the extreme bore-dom of life at sea and the intense peer pressure in an environment where the consumption of excessive amounts of 'grog' is the prime indicator of one's masculinity. Because using novels to manage alcoholism is unusual, there is a danger that too much may be made of this example. But no matter how unrepresentative of the group of readers I spoke to, and possibly read-ing more broadly, reading to 'beat the bottle' is a concrete example of the work that books can perform, a use of books that is neither immanent in the text, nor available to any textual 'reading'.

I have argued here that everyday reading is a cultural practice best conceptualised in terms of its shaping economies of practice. This formula-tion is offered as an alternative to the problematic definitions of popular or everyday reading based upon the taxonomy of texts, a unified aesthetic or a class of reader. Everyday book culture is definitely 'active', not least because reading beyond 'the pale', outside protected professional, pedagogical or aesthetic spaces, requires ingenuity on the reader's part. Readers are cer-tainly not 'cultural dupes', the much beloved whipping boys of elitist mass culture theory, and neither are they the sovereign cultural consumers uncritically imagined by cultural populists. Far from free, chaotic or anarchic, a reader's agency is circumscribed by three reading economies.

The readers clearly operate within a spatio-temporal cultural economy because reading is always an embodied experience located in time and space. Although it is possible to regard physical space as a largely inert gap within which culture just 'happens' (Soja 1989:37), the availability and type of space in which reading is performed is a constitutive element of everyday book culture. The availability of a time and space is a material restriction on every-day reading practice and within the group of readers I interviewed, time and space for reading were rarer commodities than books themselves. Without exception the readers mentioned the dearth of reading time and the lengths to which they had go to 'make time' for their books, to fit reading into their day, a day where time is always already allocated to other things. Hence to read on holiday, to read outside the daily routine, comes to represent a near utopian state, as reading without a time restriction is to escape from this particular cultural economy which, like all economies, is driven by scarcity. Holiday reading is by definition short-lived, and predictably the readers must soon return to their normal reading routine which requires them to negotiate, borrow or steal their reading time.

In finding time to read, time that is never given, a reader must also find a space for reading. Consequently, acts of every day readership often occur in liminal spaces, like the bedroom and on public transport, locations that may not even be considered 'cultural' in the conventional sense of the term. To this end, reading in one's bedroom becomes appealing because it reduces the need to negotiate the use of domestic space with others. Moreover, bedtime reading affords the silence that some readers find essential. One's bedroom is often the only location where the 'classical mode' (Steiner 1988) of reading can operate: for most metropolitan readers in the west silence and solitude are incredibly rare. In response to this lack of quiet and seclusion, a minority of the readers have developed reading practices that did not rely on their availability. These individuals' ability to read surrounded by distractions facilitates an amount of reading not possible for those who feel they must perform under the normative conditions, or not all.

If an ability to read in the communal areas of the home produces more reading, then reading on public transport has a similar effect. Reading on the bus, train or ferry, creates a cultural space, 'a place of comfort' (Wise 2000), by humanising the mundane and inescapable process of commuting. Readers use books to change their experience of commuting, to shut out the world around them, to transform if only temporarily the non-space in which they have to be. Being able to read while commuting, like reading in a crowded living room accompanied by the sounds of conversation, television or recorded music, greatly increases the amount of reading that may be undertaken and, while it may not be ideal, judged by readers' own opinions as much as by a 'universal' measure, the forty-minute bus or train trip to the office may provide the only available space for reading on that particular day.

As well as being dependent upon a particular spatio-temporal economy, everyday readership is formed by a social economy of reading. Despite the commonplace assertions to the contrary, reading is a highly social activity, learned and performed within specific social relationships. The social economy of reading is sometimes overlooked when the relations of reading are conceptualised as a straightforward dialectic between a single reader and a discrete text. Readers' first reading relationships are familial. The familial relations of reading are augmented by those of educational institutions, but outside the reading relations of the family, the school, and the college, friends provide a social network in which books are exchanged, read, valued and interpreted. The readers are, therefore, part of a number of 'proto-communities' (Willis 1990), formed through the shared consumption of a particular type of cultural text or practice.

Far from reading in social isolation, the readers are seen to rely on friends to provide books, symbolically in the form of recommendations, materially through lending and gift-giving, and discursively as 'book talk'. Reading friends are the biggest single source of reading material, far more so than the media. Within their networks of 'affectual sharing' (Maffesoli 1996), books operate as social intermediaries, their exchange enables and maintain friendships. Indeed, the exchange of books, whether symbolic, material or discursive, does not just support or facilitate the readers' friendships, they may even be thought to constitute that friendship. The exchange of books extends a reader's 'funds of sociability'—the limited resources through which cultural actors build relationships (Allen 1979)—and so facilitates a form of virtual interaction that is not dependent on face-to-face contact. The success or otherwise of a book exchange provides an index of intimacy, a measure of the solidity of a relationship. In their role as social intermediaries, books become implicated in acts of self-representation whether they are exchanged materially and symbolically, or whether they are placed on semi-public display in a bookcase or on a shelf as a marker of a life narrative. Books thus become part of a 'dispersed identity' (Marcus 1992:314).

Like the spatio-temporal economy, the social economy of everyday reading is not *there* to be read from the text. As a counter to formal and text-only studies of books, extra- or contextual approaches to culture may in some cases disregard texts completely. Despite this tendency texts may remain, as we have seen, a significant factor in cultural research without the fetishism associated with text-only approaches. The text may be re-envisaged as neither the beginning and end of meaning, nor an irrelevance, but rather as another reading economy that both facilitates and restricts readers' imaginative work: the economy of the text is the third domain of everyday reading. By conceptualising reading in terms of 'frames' or 'repertoires'(Hermes 1995; Rose 2001), the text remains a significant if not the sole object of cultural analysis. Textual analysis may be used to identify the range of possible framings of a text, which then need to be correlated with the reading practices of historically and socially situated subjects.

When reading Toni Morrison's *Beloved*, the readers framed the novel within five interpretative repertoires: biographical, autobiographical, generic, intertextual and historical. Readers' references to particular frames of interpretation do not necessarily equate to their actual readings of the text, although in some situations they might. Overall, it was the biographical frame, the production of meaning anchored in an understanding of the status and life of the author, and the historical frame, that produced the most animated and detailed discussion. This is explained by the visibility of Morrison as a literary or media star and the fact that *Beloved*'s diegetic world is related to a widely known historical event, slavery in nineteenth-century America. By comparison, the tendency to frame *Beloved* autobiographically was not as marked as could perhaps be expected as such framings are thought to require the least cultural capital. Like the biographical repertoire, the intertextual and generic frames were not particularly productive in terms of discussion, however much they may both have contributed to actual readings.

In general, these frames of interpretation do not differ entirely from those that may be deployed when reading *Beloved* within educational contexts. The desire to separate completely professional from non-professional reading at the level of narrative interpretation may be misplaced, at least within the reading practice of such educated readers. Reading is a cultural capacity that is acquired largely through an intensive and protracted relationship with educational institutions and therefore, in the case of reading, but not necessarily other everyday cultural practices, the traces of a thoroughly institutionalised cultural order may remain long after reading within formal educational contexts ceases. At the level of interpretative framings it is possible to argue that, in the case of this group of readers, there is some degree of intersection or overlap between scholarly and everyday economies of the text.

For analytical purposes, I have separated the everyday reading economy into three separate cultural zones. However, as the readers' discourse makes clear, everyday reading always occurs within all three economies *simultaneously*: readers are always reading a particular text with a particular form, in a particular place and within a particular social relationship. All cultural practices, as Raymond Williams suggests, are always 'in solution ... known, if often indistinctly and unevenly, as whole and connected' (Williams 1977:140). So if cultural accounts are serious in their attempts to represent the complexity of cultural life in media-saturated societies, then an attempt to recognise, account for and analyse these connections is crucial. The desire to see reading as a thoroughly embedded cultural practice rather than a largely cognitive relationship between a solitary reader and a singular text made a change in research method a necessity. Indeed, with the help of the readers themselves, the conception of everyday that I have related here would not have been possible without such a methodological shift.

As my formulation of everyday reading is one based in particular practices rather than specific types of texts, an analytical method like textual analysis, unadorned, is no longer an appropriate choice of research tool. To approach these non-professional reading practices, researchers need to go beyond the text and textual analysis, to refrain from reading the text as if its boundaries formed the limits of the culturally meaningful, and supplement text-only analysis with an ethnographic or qualitative method which 'is based on trying to understand how texts make sense to others, in the context of their lives' (Hermes 1995:147). Ethnographic or qualitative methodologies have themselves been subject to rigorous analysis in recent decades. However, rather than diminish the appeal of the method, ethnographers may now produce ethnographic accounts with an increased awareness of their method's methodological, epistemological and ethical limits. This renewed methodological awareness has perhaps strengthened the method against the attacks of its detractors, and in so doing the traditional strengths of ethnographic method have remained.

To resist reading the *textual* as if it were the *cultural* requires researchers to surrender some control over their research. The researcher has to be prepared to go where the material leads them, even if that material steers them away from a preferred or preconfigured destination. By augmenting textual analysis with an ethnographic method, researchers may create a forum in which the voices of cultural actors, albeit mediated, may be heard where otherwise they would be silent, or silenced. In such qualitative methods, researchers should strive 'to listen "through" the text for the resonance of its everyday use' (Hermes 1995:148). This act of listening also applies to the cultural narratives, the stories of reading, provided by ethnographic subjects themselves. Listening is always significant in qualitative research but even more so for projects that rely on interview material rather than the more traditional and prolonged participant observation.

This change in research method from textual analysis to 'thick' (Geertz 1973) or 'broad' description (Becker 1986), allows researchers to construct different accounts of everyday reading culture based, not just on specific texts, but particular practices. Certainly, the stories of everyday reading given by my readers have shaped the story of everyday reading offered by this book. Whereas text-only criticism often has a tendency to treat the novel, play or poem as metaphor *for* culture, ethnographic or qualitative accounts are adept at placing texts and their accompanying practices in a wider cultural and social world: the world *in* the text is exchanged for the text *in* the world. If they resist the temptation to read the world *from* the text, and the allied assumption that everything significant about a cultural artefact may be decoded through the application of the right theory, researchers may counter the orientalising tendency of all cultural representation by exchanging 'the textual attitude' for 'the disorientations of direct encounters with the human' (Said 1980:112). By surrendering some of our discursive power as researchers, a power that is implicit in textual fetishism, we may come to understand the way in which books are used by the many, rather than how they are read by the few.

List of References

Abrams, M.H. (1999) *A Glossary of Literary Terms*, 7th ed., Fort Worth: Harcourt Brace College

Abu-Lughod, L. (1999) 'The Interpretation of Culture(s) after Television', in Sherry Ortner (ed) *The Fate of "Culture": Geertz and Beyond*, Berkeley: University of California

Adams, R. and Allen, G. (1998) (eds) *Placing Friendship in Context*, Cambridge: Cambridge University Press

Agar, M. (1986) *Speaking of Ethnography*, Beverley Hills: Sage

Alcoff, L. (1991) 'The Problem of Speaking for Others', in *Cultural Critique* winter: 5-32

Allen, G. (1979) *A Sociology of Friendship and Kinship*, London: Allen & Unwin

Allen, G. (1998) 'Friendship and the Private Sphere', in R. Adams and G. Allen (eds) *Placing Friendship in Context*, London: Cambridge University Press

Altick, R. (1963) *The English Common Reader*, Chicago: Phoenix

Ang, I. (1982) *Watching Dallas*, London: Methuen

Ang, I. (1996) *Living Room Wars: Rethinking Media Audiences for a Postmodern World*, London: Routledge

Arnold, M. (1973) 'Culture and Anarchy', in G. Sutherland (ed) *Arnold on Education*, London: Penguin

Ashley, B. (1997) (ed) *Reading Popular Narrative: A Source Book*, London: Leicester University Press

Australian Bureau of Statistics, (1992) *Time Use on Culture/Leisure Activities*, Canberra: AGPS

Australian Centre for Youth Literature, (2001) *Young Australians Reading: From Keen to Reluctant Reader*, Sydney: Woolcott Research

Australia Council for the Arts, (2001) *Books Alive! A National Survey of Reading, Buying and Borrowing Books for Pleasure*, Sydney: AC Nielsen

Baker, S. (2001) '"Welcome to the Easy Mix with Mandy as your Host": Radio Play in the Bedrooms of Pre-Teen Girls', in D. Crowdy, S. Homan and T. Mitchell (eds) *Musical In-Between-Ness, The Proceedings of the 8th IASPM Australian New Zealand Conference*, Sydney: IASPM & UTS

Barker, M. (1997) 'Taking the Extreme Case: Understanding a Fascist Fan of Judge Dredd', in Hunter, I.Q. et. al. (ed) *Trash Aesthetics: Popular Culture and its Audience*, London: Pluto Press

Baron, N. (2000) *Alphabet to Email: How Written English Evolved and Where it's Heading*, London and New York: Routledge

Barthes, R. (1984) *Image, Music, Text*, London: Flamingo

Barthes, R. (1988) 'The Death of the Author', in D. Lodge (ed) *Modern Criticism and Theory*, London: Longman

Barton, D, and Hamilton, M. (1998) *Local Literacies: Reading and Writing in One Community*, London: Routledge

Basbanes, N.J. (2005) *Every Book its Reader: The Power of the Printed Word to Stir the World*, New York: Harper Perennial

Batsleer, J. (1997) 'Pulp in the Pink', in B. Ashley (ed) *Reading Popular Narrative*, London: Leicester University Press

Batsleer, J., Davies, T., O' Rourke, R. and Weedon, C. (1985) *Rewriting English: Cultural Politics of Gender and Class*, London: Methuen

Bayard, P. (2007) *How to Talk About Books You Haven't Read*, New York: Bloomsbury USA

Bayer, A. (2001) 'Consuming History and Memory through Mass Media Products', in *European Journal of Cultural Studies* 4, 4: 491-501

Becker, H. (1982) *Art Worlds*, Berkeley: University of California Press

Becker, H. (1986) 'Telling About Society', in H. Becker *Doing Things Together*, Evanston: North-West Uni Press [www.lsweb.sscf.ucsb/depts/soc/faculty/ hbecker/Telling_paper.html:30/6/200]

Becker, H. (1996) 'The Epistemology of Qualitative Research', in R. Jessor, A. Colby, and R. Schweder (eds) *Essays on Ethnography and Human Development*, Chicago: University of Chicago Press, [www.lsweb.sscf.ucsb/depts/soc/faculty/hbecker/ qa.html: 30/6/200]

Belsey, C. (1980) *Critical Practice*, London: Methuen

Benjamin, W. (1992) *Illuminations*, London: Fontana

Bennett, T. (1988) *Outside Literature*, London: Routledge

Bennett, T., Frow, J., and Emmison M., (1999) *Accounting For Tastes: Australia Everyday Cultures*, Cambridge: Cambridge University Press

Bennett, T., and Woollacott, J. (1987) *Bond And Beyond: the Political Career of a Popular Hero*, Houndmills: Macmillan

Berman, M. (1983) *All That is Solid Melts into Air: The Experience of Modernity*, London: Verso

Birkerts, S. (1994) *The Gutenberg Elegies: the Fate of Reading in an Electronic Age*, Boston: Faber and Faber

Bloom, A. (1984) *The Closing of the American Mind,* London: Penguin

Bloom, H. (1994) *The Western Canon*, New York: Papermac

Bloom, H. (2001) *How to Read and Why*, London: Fourth Estate

Bourdieu, P. (1984) *Distinction: A Social Critique of the Judgement of Taste*, London: Routledge & Keegan Paul

Boxall, P. (2005) *1001 Books You Must Read Before You Die*, London: Universe

Boyarin, J. (1993) (ed) *The Ethnography of Reading*, Berkeley: University of California Press

Bragg, M. (2006) *12 Books that Changed the World*, London: Hodder & Stoughton

British Broadcasting Corporation (2008) 'World Book Club', *BBC Online* [www.bbc.co.uk/worldservice/specials/133_wbc_archive_new: 11/10/07]

Brown, M.E. (1996) '"Desperately Seeking Strategies": Reading in the Postmodern World', in D. Grodin and T. Lindlof (eds) *Constructing the Self in a Mediated World*, Thousand Oaks: Sage

Buckingham, D. (1993) (ed) *Reading Audiences: Young People and the Media*, Manchester: Manchester University Press

Buckridge, P., Murray, P. and MaCleod, J. (1995) *Reading Professional Identities: The Boomers and their Books*, Griffith: ICPS, Griffith University

Bull, M. (2000) *Sounding Out the City: Personal Stereos and the Management of Everyday Life*, Oxford: Berg

Burke, P. (1978) *Popular Culture in Early Modern Europe*, London: Temple Smith

Carter, D. (2001) 'Public Intellectuals, Book Culture and Civil Society', in *Australian Humanities Review*, December, [www.lib.latrobe.edu.au/AHR/archive/Issue-December-2001/carter2.html]

Carter, D. (2008) 'Book Culture without Books', in *Australian Humanities Review*, March, [www.australianhumanitiesreview.org/archive/Issue-March-2008/carter.html]

Cartmell, D., Kaye, H., Whelehan , I. and Hunter, I.Q. (1997) (eds) *Trash Aesthetics: Popular Culture and its Audience*, London: Pluto Press

Cavallo, G. and Chartier, R. (1999) 'Introduction', in G. Cavallo and R. Chartier (eds) *A History of Reading in the West*, Cambridge: Polity Press

Cavallo, G. and Chartier, R. (1999) (ed) *A History of Reading in the West*, Cambridge: Polity Press

Cavicchi, D. (1998) *Tramps Like Us*, New York: Oxford University Press

Cawelti, J. (1986) 'Review of *Reading The Romance*', in *American Journal of Sociology* 91, May: 1512-13

Chabot Davis, K. (2004) 'Oprah's Book Club and the Politics of Cross-Racial Empathy', in *International Journal of Cultural Studies*, 7, 4:339-417

Chambers, I. (1986) *Popular Culture: The Metropolitan Experience*, New York: Methuen

Chartier, R. (1995) *Forms and Meanings*, Philadelphia: University of Pennsylvania Press

Cherland, M. (1994) *Private Practices: Critical Perspectives on Literacy and Education*, London: Taylor & Francis

Christian, B. (1993) 'Fixing Methodologies: *Beloved*' in *Cultural Critique*, Spring: 5-15

Clifford, J. (1986) 'Introduction', in J. Clifford and G. Marcus, G. (eds) *Writing Culture: the Poetics and Politics of Ethnography*, Berkeley: University of California Press

Clifford, J. and Marcus, G. (1986) (eds) *Writing Culture: the Poetics & Politics of Ethnography*, Berkeley: University of California Press

Cloonan, M. (1997) 'Class Acts? Taste and Popular Music', paper given at the International Association for the Study of Popular Music Conference, Kanazawa, Japan: IASPM

Cobley, P. (2001) *Narrative*, Routledge: London

Cohen, S. (1991) *Rock Culture in Liverpool: Popular Music in the Making*, New York: Clarendon Press

Colebrook, C. (1997) *New Literary Histories: New Histories and Contemporary Criticism*, Manchester: Manchester University Press

Collins, J. (1989) *Uncommon Cultures: Popular Culture and Post-Modernism*, New York and London: Routledge

Collins, S. (1992) (ed) *Interpretation and Overinterpretation*, Cambridge: Cambridge University Press

Connor, S. (1997) *Postmodernist Culture: an Introduction to Theories of the Contemporary*, 2nd ed, London: Blackwells

Corner, J. (1983) 'Textuality, Communication and Media Power', in H. Davis and P. Walton (eds) *Language, Image, Media*, Oxford: Blackwell

Couldry, N. (2000) *The Place of Media Power: Pilgrims and Witness of the Media Age*, London: Routledge

Coupland, J. and Gwyn, R. (2003) (eds) *Discourse, the Body and Identity*, London: Macmillan/Palgrave

Crang, M. (1998) *Cultural Geography*, London and New York: Routledge

Cranney-Francis, A. (1995) *The Body in the Text*, Melbourne: Melbourne University Press

Crick, M. and Geddes, B. (1998) 'Introduction', in M. Crick and B. Geddes, B. (eds) *Research Methods in the Field: Eleven Anthropological Accounts*, 2nd ed, Geelong (Victoria): Deakin University Press

Crick, M. and Geddes, B. (1998) (eds) *Research Methods in the Field: Eleven Anthropological Accounts*, 2nd ed, Geelong (Victoria): Deakin University Press

Crowdy, D., Homan, S. and Bennett, T. (2001) (eds) *Musical In-Between-Ness, The Proceedings of the 8th IASPM Australian New Zealand Conference*, Sydney: IASPM & UTS

Cullen, J. (1998) *Born in the USA: Bruce Springsteen and the American Tradition*, New York: Harper

Curran, J. (2002) *Media and Power*, London: Routledge

Curran, J. and Gurevitch, M. (1995) (eds) *Mass Media and Society*, London: Edward Arnold

Dant, T. (1999) *Material Culture in the Social World*, Buckingham: Open University Press

David, R. (2000) *Toni Morrison Explained: A Reader's Road Map to the Novels*, New York: Random House

de Certeau, M. (1984) *The Practice of Everyday Life*, Berkeley: University of California Press

de Certeau, M. (1997) *Culture in the Plural*, Minneapolis: University of Minnesota Press

De Grazia, S. (1962) *Of Time, Work and Leisure*, Anchor Books: New York

Docker, J. (1994) *Postmodernism and Popular Culture: A Cultural History*, Cambridge: Cambridge University Press

Donahue, D. (1987) 'The Lyrical World of Toni Morrison', in *Bookshelf: USA Today* [http://www.usatoday.com/life/enter/books/oprah/o003htm: 11/09/2000]

Douglas, M. and Isherwood, B. (1996) *The World of Goods: Towards an Anthropology of Consumption*, London: Routledge

Drotner, K. (1994) 'Ethnographic Enigmas: "The Everyday" in Recent Media Studies', in *Cultural Studies* 8, 2: 341-357

During, S. (1990) 'Professing the Popular', in *Meanjin*, 3, 49: 481-91

During, S. (1993) (ed) *The Cultural Studies Reader*, 1st ed., London: Routledge

During, S. (1999) 'Introduction', in S. During (ed) *The Cultural Studies Reader,* 2nd ed., London: Routledge

During, S. (1999) (ed) *The Cultural Studies Reader*, 2nd ed., London: Routledge

Eagleton, T. (1983) *Literary Theory: An Introduction*, London: Blackwells

Eco, U. (1992) 'Between Author and Text', in S. Collins (ed) *Interpretation and Overinterpretation*, Cambridge: Cambridge University Press.

Eipper, C. (1998) 'Anthropology and Cultural Studies: Difference, Ethnography and Theory', in *The Australian Journal of Anthropology* 9, 3: 310-26

Elam, D. (1995) 'Speak for Yourself', in J. Roff and R. Wiegnam (eds) *Who Can Speak? Authority and Critical Identity*, Urbana: University of Illinois

Eliot, S. and Owens, W.R. (1998) (eds) *A Handbook to Literary Research*, London: Routledge and Open University Press

Elsner, J. and Cardinal, R. (1994) (eds) *The Culture of Collecting*, Melbourne: Melbourne University Press

Falconer, D.(2007) 'Left With a Sense of Longing', in *The Australian Literary Review*, August, 6-7/10

Ferguson, M. and Golding, P. (1997) (eds) *Cultural Studies in Question*, London: Sage

Fischer, S.R. (2003) *A History of Reading*, London: Reaktion

Fish, S. (1980) *Is There a Text in this Class?*, Cambridge (Mass): Harvard University Press

Fiske, J. (1989) *Understanding Popular Culture*, London: Unwin Hyman

Fleishman, A. (1978) *Fiction and the Ways of Knowing*, Austin and London: University of Texas Press

Forgacs, D. (1992) 'Marxist Literary Theory', in A. Jefferson, and D. Robey (eds) *Modern Literary Theory: A Comparative Introduction* 2nd ed., Batsford: London

Foucault, M. (1988) 'What is an Author?' in D. Lodge (ed) *Modern Criticism and Theory*, Harlow: Longman

Fowles, J. (1996) *Advertising and Popular Culture*, London: Sage

Frankel, B. (1992) *From Prophets Deserts Come*, Melbourne: Arena

Frow, J. (1997) *Time and Commodity Culture: Essays in Cultural Theory and Postmodernity*, Oxford: Oxford University Press

Frith, S. (1991) 'The Good, the Bad and the Indifferent: Defending Popular Culture', in *Diacrtics* 21, 4: 102-15

Frow, J. (1996) *Cultural Studies and Cultural Value*, Oxford: Clarendon Press

Game, A. and Metcalfe, A. (1998) *Passionate Sociology*, London: Sage

Ganguly-Scrase, R. (1998) 'The Self as Research Instrument', in M. Crick and B. Geddes (eds) *Research Methods in the Field: Eleven Anthropological Accounts*, 2nd ed., Geelong (Victoria): Deakin University Press

Gass, W. (1999) 'In Defense of Books: Why Books are Good', in *Harper's Magazine* [http://www.findarticles.com/p/articles/mi_m/is_1794_299/ai_57155717/print: 20/11/07]

Geertz, C. (1973) *The Interpretations of Cultures*, USA: Basic Books

Geraghty, C. (1998) 'Audiences and Ethnography: Questions of Practice', in C. Geraghty and K. Lusted (eds) *The Television Studies Book*, London: Arnold

Geraghty, C. and Lusted, K. (1998) (eds) *The Television Studies Book*, London: Arnold

Giddens, A. (1990) *The Consequences of Modernity*, London: Polity Press

Giddens, A. (1991) *Modernity and Self Identity*, London: Polity Press

Gilroy, P. (1993) *Small Acts Thoughts on the Politics of Black Cultures*, London: Serpent's Tail

Goffman, E. (1959) *The Presentation of Self in Everyday Life*, Harmondsworth: Penguin

Goffman, E. (1975) *Frame Analysis: An Essay on the Organisation of Experience*, Harmondsworth: Penguin

Golding, P. and Murdock, G. (1995) 'Culture, Communications, and Political Economy', in J. Curran and M. Gurevitch (eds) *Mass Media and Society*, London: Edward Arnold

Graubard, S. (1983) (ed) *Reading in the 1980s*, New York: Bowker

Gray, A. (1997) 'Learning From Experience', in J. McGuigan (ed) *Cultural Methodologies*, London: Sage

Greaney, V. and Hegarty, M. (1987) 'Correlates of Leisure-Time Reading' in *Journal of Research in Reading* 10, 1: 3-20

Green, E. et al (1990) *Women's Leisure, What Leisure?*, London: Macmillan

Grimshaw, R., Hobson, D. and Willis, P. (1980) 'Introduction to Ethnography at the Centre', in S. Hall (ed) *Culture, Media, Language*, London: Hutchison and the Centre for Contemporary Cultural Studies

Grodin, D. and Lindlof, T. (1996) (eds) *Constructing the Self in a Mediated World*, Thousand Oaks: Sage

Guldberg, G. (1990) *Books—Who Reads Them?*, Redfern (NSW): Australia Council

Hall, S. (1980) (ed) *Culture, Media, Language*, London: Hutchison and the Centre for Contemporary Cultural Studies

Hall, S. (1994) 'Notes on Deconstructing the "Popular"', in J. Storey (ed) *Cultural Theory and Popular Culture: a Reader*, Hemel Hempstead: Harvester/Wheatsheaf

Hall, S. (1997) (ed) *Representations: Cultural Representations and Signifying Practices*, London: Open University Press

Hall, S. (1999) 'Cultural Studies and its Theoretical Legacies', in S. During (ed) *The Cultural Studies Reader*, 2nd ed., London: Routledge

Hall, S. and Jeffersen, T. (1976) (eds) *Resistance through Rituals: Youth Subcultures in Post-War Britiain*, London: Hutchison and the Centre for Contemporary Cultural Studies

Hammersley, M. (1992) *What's Wrong With Ethnography?*, London: Routledge

Hammersley, M. and Atkinson, P. (1983) *Ethnography: Principles in Practice*, London: Tavistock

Harrison, K. (1998) 'Rich Friendships, Affluent Friends: Middle-Class Practices of Friendship', in R. Adams and G. Allen (eds) *Placing Friendship in Context*, London: Cambridge University Press

Henderson, K., Bialeschki, M., Shaw, S. and Freysinger, V. (1989) *A Leisure of One's Own: A Feminist Perspective on Leisure*, London: Routledge

Hermes, J. (1995) *Reading Women's Magazines: An Analysis of Everyday Media Use*, Cambridge: Polity Press

Hermes, J. (2000) 'Cultural Citizenship and Crime Fiction', in *European Journal of Cultural Studies* 3, 2: 215-32

Hobbs, D. and May, T. (1993) *Interpreting the Field: Accounts of Ethnography*, Oxford: Oxford University Press

Hobson, D. (1982) *Crossroads: The Drama of Soap Opera*, London: Methuen

Hoggart, R. (1957) *The Uses of Literacy*, Harmondsworth: Penguin

Hoggart, R. (1970) *Speaking to Each Other, Vol. 2*, Ringwood: Penguin

Hoggart, R. (1999) *First and Last Things*, London Aurum

Inglis, F. (1988) *Popular Culture and Political Power*, New York: St. Martin's Press

Iser, W. (1988) 'The Reading Process: A Phenomenological Approach', in D. Lodge (ed) *Modern Criticism and Theory*, Harlow: Longman

Jackman, C. (1999) 'US Literati Honour Their Contentious Hero Oprah', in *The Sunday Telegraph*, 14/11/99

James, W. (1978) *Pragmatism and the Meaning of Truth*, Cambridge (Mass): Harvard University Press

Jameson, F. (1991) *Postmodern: The Cultural Logic of Late-Capitalism*, London: Verso

Jankowski, N. and Wester, F. (1992) 'The Qualitative Tradition in Social Science Inquiry: Contributions to Mass Communications Research', in K.B. Jenson and N. Jankowski (eds) *A Handbook of Qualitative Methods for Mass Communications Research*, London: Routledge

Jefferson, A. and Robey, D. (1992) *Modern Literary Theory: A Comparative Introduction*, 2nd ed., London: Batsford

Jenkins, H. (1992) *Textual Poachers*, London: Routledge

Jensen, J. (1990) *Redeeming Modernity: Contradiction in Media Criticism*, London: Sage

Jensen, J. (1992) 'Fandom as Pathology: The Consequences of Characterisation', in L. Lewis (ed) *The Adoring Audiences: Fan Culture and Popular Media*, London: Routledge

Jensen, J. and Pauly, J. (1997) 'Imaging the Audience: Losses and Gains in Cultural Studies', in M. Ferguson and P. Golding (eds) *Cultural Studies in Question*, London: Sage

Jenson, K.B. and Jankowski, N. (1992) (eds) *A Handbook of Qualitative Methods for Mass Communications Research*, London: Routledge

Johnson, B. (1998) 'Watching the Watcher: Who Do We Think We Are? "Knowing Popular Music"' [http://www.arts.unsw.edu.au/jazz/Arch/BJAR/Watching_the_watchers.htm: 2/01/2000]

Johnson, B. (2000) *The Inaudible Music: Jazz, Gender and Australia Modernity*, Sydney: Currency Press

Johnson, R. (1987) "What is Cultural Studies Anyway?', in *Social Text* 16, 1: 38-80

Kellner, D. (1995) *Media Culture*, London: Routledge

Knauft, B. (1994) '"Pushing Anthropology Past the Post": Critical Notes on Cultural Anthropology and Cultural Studies as Influenced by Postmodernism and Existentialism', in *Critique of Anthropology* 14, 2: 152-77

Korhonen, K. (2006) 'Textual: Nancy, Blanchot, Derrida', in *Culture Machine* 8, [www.culturemachine.tees.ac.uk/Cmach?Backissues/j008/journal.htm: 2/4/08]

Lash, S. and Friedman, J. (eds) (1992) *Modernity and Identity*, London: Blackwell

Leavis, F.R. (1948) *The Great Tradition*, London: Penguin

Leavis, Q.D. (1932) *Fiction and the Reading Public*, London: Chatto & Windus

Lefebvre, H. (1991) *Critique of Everyday Life*, London: Verso

Lewis, L. (1992) (ed) *The Adoring Audiences: Fan Culture and Popular Media*, London: Routledge

Lodge, D. (1988) (ed) *Modern Criticism and Theory*, London: Longman

Long, E. (1987) 'Reading Groups and the Postmodern Crisis of Cultural Authority', in *Cultural Studies* 1, 1: 306-27

Long, E. (1993) 'Textual Interpretation as Collective Action', in J. Boyarin (ed) *The Ethnography of Reading*, Berkeley: University of California Press

Long, E. (2003) *Book Clubs: Women and Uses of Reading in Everyday Life*, London and Chicago: University of Chicago Press

Lovatt, A. and Purkis, J. (1995) 'Shouting in the Street: Popular Culture, Values, and the New Ethnography', *Institute for Popular Culture*, Manchester: Manchester Metropolitan University [http://darion.mmu.ac.uk/h&ss/mipc/ethno1.htm: 15/07/99]

Lovell, T. (1987) *Consuming Fiction*, London: Verso

Lyons, M. (1992) 'Texts, Books, and Readers: Which Kind of Cultural History?', in *Australian Cultural History* 11: 1-5

Lyons, M. (1998) 'New Readers in the Nineteenth Century: Women, Children, Workers', in G. Cavallo and R. Chartier (eds) *A History of Reading in the West*, Cambridge: Polity Press

Lyons, M. (2001) 'Reading Models and Reading Communities', in M. Lyons and J. Arnold (eds) *A History of Book in Australia 1891-1945: A National Culture in a Colonised Market*, St. Lucia (QLD): University of Queensland Press

Lyons, M. and Arnold, J. (2001) (eds) *A History of Book in Australia 1891-1945: A National Culture in a Colonised Market*, St. Lucia (QLD): University of Queensland Press

Lyons, M. and Taksa, L. (1992) 'If Mother Caught us Reading ... ! Impressions of the Australian Woman Reader 1890-1933', in *Australian Cultural History* 11:39-50

McCarthy, J. (2002) 'The Mother of All Book Clubs', in *Spectrum*, Jan 5-6: 8-9

McCrum, R. (2008) 'A Thriller in Ten Chapters', in *The Guardian Online*, May 25 [http://books.guardian.co.uk/print/0,,334366068-99930,00.htm: accessed 8/6/08]

McDowell, L. and Pringle, R. (1992) *Defining Women*, Cambridge: Polity Press

McEachern, C. (1998) 'A Mutual Interest? Ethnography in Anthropology and Cultural Studies', in *The Australian Journal of Anthropology* 9, 3: 251-64

McGuigan, J. (1992) *Cultural Populism*, London: Routledge

McGuigan, J. (1997) (ed) *Cultural Methodologies*, London: Sage

McKernan, S. (1990) 'Female Literacy and Male Success: the Implication of Gendered Reading', in J. Macleod and P. Buckridge (eds) *Books and Reading in Australia*, Griffith (QLD): Institute of Cultural Policy Studies, Griffith University

MacLachlan, G. and Reid, I. (1994) *Framing and Interpretation*, Melbourne: Melbourne University Press

MacLeod, J. and Buckridge, P. (eds) (1992) *Books and Reading in Australian Society*, Griffith (QLD): Institute of Cultural Policy Studies, Griffith University

McRobbie, A. (1997) (ed) *Back To Reality*, Manchester: Manchester University Press

McRobbie, A. and Garber, R. (1976) 'Girls and Subcultures': An Exploration', in S. Hall and T. Jefferson (eds) *Resistance through Rituals*, London: Hutchison and the Centre for Contemporary Cultural Studies

Maffesoli, M. (1996) *The Time of the Tribes: The End of Individualism and the Mass Society*, London: Sage

Malinowski, B. (1974) *Magic, Science and Religion*, London: Sourein Press

Mandel Morrow, L. (1995) (ed) *Family Literacies: Connections in Schools and Communities*, New Brunswick: Rutgers University Press

Manguel, A. (1996) *A History of Reading*, New York: Viking

Mann, P. (1971) *Books, Buyers and Borrowers*, London: Andre Deutsch

Marcus, G. (1992) 'Past, Present and Emergent Identities: Requirements for Ethnographies of Late Twentieth-Century Modernity Worldwide', in S. Lash and J. Friedman (ed) *Modernity and Identity*, London: Blackwells

Marks, V. (1994) 'Objects and Their Maker: Bricolage of the Self', in S. H. Riggins (ed) *The Socialness of Things: Essays on the Socio-Semiotics of Objects*, Berlin: de Gruyter

Marshall, P.D. (1994) *Celebrity and Power: Fame in Contemporary Culture*, Minnesota: University of Minnesota Press

Martin, W. (1986) *Recent Theories of Narrative*, Ithaca: Cornell University Press

Mauss, M. (1967) *The Gift: Forms and Functions of Exchange in Archaic Societies*, New York: Norton

Mayer, R. (1997) *History and the Early English Novel*, London: Cambridge University Press: London

Meyrowitz, J. (1988) *No Sense of Place: The Impact of Electronic Media on Social Behaviour*, Oxford and New York: Oxford University Press

Miall, D. S. (2006) 'Empirical Approaches to Studying Literary Readers: the State of the Discipline', in *Book History* 9 :291-311

Milner, A. (1993) *Cultural Materialism*, Melbourne: Melbourne University Press Melbourne

Milner, A. (2005) *Literature, Culture and Society*, 2nd ed., Abingdon: Routledge

Moglan, H. (1993) 'Redeeming History: Toni Morrison's *Beloved*', in *Cultural Critique* Spring: 17-40

Moran, J. (2000) *Star Authors: Literary Celebrity in America*, London: Pluto Press

Morgan, C. (2007) 'The Good Read', in Spectrum, *Sydney Morning Herald* [http://hyperhub.com.au/library/images/spectrum.jpg: 23/01/08]

Morley, D. (1980) *The Nationwide Audience*, London: BFI

Morley, D. (1986) *Family Television: Cultural Power and Domestic Leisure*, London: Comedia

Morley, D. (1997) 'Theoretical Orthodoxies: Textualism, Constructivism and the "New Ethnographies"', in M. Ferguson and P. Golding (eds) *Cultural Studies in Question*, London: Sage

Morley, D. and Silverstone, R. (1990) 'Domestic Communication—Technologies and Meanings', in *Media, Culture and Society* 12: 31-55

Morley, D. and Silverstone, R. (1992) 'Communication and Context': Ethnographic Perspectives on the Media Audience', in K.B. Jenson and N. Jankowski (eds) *A Handbook of Qualitative Methods for Mass Communications Research*, London: Routledge

Morris, M. (1988) 'Banality in Cultural Studies' in *Block*, 14 [www.kuenstlerhaus.de/haus.0/SCRIPT/txt1999/11/Morrise.html.HTML:24/7/ 2001]

Morrison, T. (1990) 'Rootedness: The Ancestor as Foundation', in D. Walder (ed.) *Literature in the Modern World: Critical Essays and Documents*, Oxford: Oxford University Press

Morrison, T. (1993) (ed) *Race-ing, Justice, Engendering Power: Essays on Anita Hill, Clarence Thomas, and the Construction of Social Reality*, London: Chatto & Windus

Morrison, T. (1997) *Beloved*, London: Vintage

Morrison, T., and Lacour, C.B. (1997) (eds) *Birth of a Nationhood: Gaze, Script, and Spectacle in the O.J. Simpson Case*, New York: Pantheon

Moss, G. (1993) 'Girls Tell the Teen Romance: Four Reading Histories' in D. Buckingham (ed) *Reading Audiences: Young People and the Media*, Manchester: Manchester University Press

Muecke, S. (1993) 'Studying the Other: A Dialogue with a Postgrad', in *Cultural Studies 7*, 2: 324-29

Muensterberger, W. (1994) *Collecting: An Unruly Passion*, New Jersey: Princeton University Press

Munslow, A. (1997) *Deconstructing History*, London: Routledge

Murdock, G. (1997) 'Cultural Studies at the Crossroads', in A. McRobbie (ed) *Back to Reality: Social Experience: Social Experience and Cultural Studies*, Manchester: Manchester University Press

Nafisi, A. (2003) *Reading Lolita in Tehran,* Hodder: Sydney

National Endowment for the Arts (2004) *Reading at Risk: A Survey of Literary Reading in America*, Research Division Report No. 46, Washington

Nightingale, V. (1993) 'What's "Ethnographic" about Ethnographic Audience Research', in S. During (ed) *The Cultural Studies Reader*, 1st ed., London: Routledge

Nightingale, V. (1996) *Studying Audiences: The Shock of the Real*, London: Routledge

Norris, C. (1997) *Deconstruction: Theory and Practice*, London: Routledge

Nussbaum, M. (1995) *Poetic Justice: The Literary Imagination and Public Life*, Boston, Beacon Press

O'Connor, P. (1992) *Friendship between Women: A Critical Review*, London Harvester/ Wheatsheaf: London

O'Connor, P. (1998) 'Women's Friendships in a Post-Modern World', in R. Adams and G. Allen, (eds) *Placing Friendship in Context*, Cambridge: Cambridge University Press

Oliker, S.J. (1998) 'The Modernisation of Friendship: Individualism, Intimacy, and Gender in the Nineteenth Century', in R. Adams and G. Allen, (eds) *Placing Friendship in Context*, Cambridge: Cambridge University Press

Ortner, S. (1999) (ed) *The Fate of "Culture": Geertz and Beyond*, Berkeley: University of California

Parkin, W. (2001) 'Oprah Winfrey's Change Your Life TV and the Spiritual Everyday', in *Continuum: Journal of Media and Cultural Studies 15*, 2: 145-57

Patrick, B.A. (2008) 'Vikings and Rappers: The Icelandic Sagas Hip-Hop Across 8 Mile', in *The Journal of Popular Culture*, 1, 2: 281-305

Peck, J. (2000) 'Literacy, Seriousness, and the Oprah Winfrey Book Club', in C. Sparks and J. Tulloch (eds) *Tabloid Tales: Global Debates Over Media Standards*, New York: Rowan & Littlefield

Penley, C. (1989) *The Future of an Illusion: Film, Feminism and Psychoanalysis*, Minneapolis: University of Minnesota Press

Petrucci, A. (1999) 'Reading to Read: A Future for Reading', in G. Cavallo and R. Chartier (eds) *A History of Reading in the West*, Cambridge: Polity Press Cambridge

Plasa, C. (ed) (2000) *Toni Morrison Beloved: A Reader's Guide to Essential Criticism*, Oxford: Icon Books

Plummer, K. (1995) *Telling Sexual Stories: Power, Change and Social Worlds*, London: Routledge

Porter Abbott, H. (2002) *The Cambridge Introduction to Narrative*, Cambridge: Cambridge University Press

Postman, N. (1985) *Amusing Ourselves to Death*, New York: Viking

Radway, J. (1984/1991) *Reading the Romance: Women, Patriarchy and Popular Culture*, Chapel Hill: University of North Carolina Press

Radway, J. (1988) 'Reception Study: Ethnography and the Problem of Dispersed Audiences and Nomadic Subjects', in *Cultural Studies* 2, 3: 358-79

Regan, S. (1998) 'Reader-Response Criticism and Reception Theory', in S. Eliot and W.R. Owens (eds) *A Handbook to Literary Research*, London: Routledge and Open University Press

Repplier, A. (1891) 'English Railway Fiction', Cornell University: *Making of America*, On-line Collection [http://cdl.library.cornell.edu: 26/03/2001]

Richardson, L. (1995) 'Narrative and Sociology', in J. Van Maanen (ed) *Representation in Ethnography*, London: Sage

Riggins, S.H. (1994) 'Fieldwork in the Living Room: an Autobiographical Essay', in S. H. Riggins (ed) *The Socialness of Things: Essays on the Socio- Semiotics of Objects*, Berlin: de Gruyter

Riggins, S.H. (1994) (ed) *The Socialness of Things: Essays on the Socio-Semiotics of Objects*, Berlin: de Gruyter

Roff, J. and Wiegnam, R. (1995) (eds) *Who Can Speak? Authority and Critical Identity*, Urbana: University of Illinois

Rorty, R. (1992) 'The Pragmatist's Progress', in S. Collins (ed) *Interpretation and Overinterpretation*, Cambridge: Cambridge University Press

Rorty, R. (2002) 'Words or Words Apart? The Consequences of Pragmatism For Literary Studies: An Interview with Richard Rorty', with E.P. Ragg, in *Philosophy and Literature*, 26:369-96

Rose, J. (2001) *The Intellectual Life of the British Working Class*, New Haven: Yale University Press

Rowse, T. (1985) *Arguing the Arts*, Ringwood: Penguin

Rutz, H. (1992) 'Introduction: The Idea of a Politics of Time', in H. Rutz (ed) *The Politics of Time*, Washington, DC: American Ethnological Society

Rutz, H. (1992) (ed) *The Politics of Time*, Washington, DC: American Ethnological Society

Said, E. (1980) *Orientalism*, London: Routledge & Keegan Paul

Samuel, R. (1994) *Past and Present in Contemporary Culture*, London: Verso

Sapsford, R. and Jupp, V. (1992) (eds) *Data Collection and Analysis*, London: Sage and Open University Press

Sartre, J.-P. (1981) *Nausea*, Harmondsworth: Penguin

Sarup, M. (1996) *Identity, Culture and the Postmodern World*, Edinburgh: Edinburgh University Press

Sawhill, R. (1999) 'Unrequired Reading' in *Salon.com* [http://www.salon.com/book/feature/1999/07/16/pubpros: 20/8/99]

Schivelbusch, W. (1986) *The Railway Journey: the Industrialisation of Time and Space in the Nineteenth Century*, London: Berg

Schrevders, P. (1981) *The Book of Paperbacks: a Visual History of the Paperback Book*, London: Virgin Books

Seiter, E. (1999) *Television and New Media Audiences*, Oxford: Clarendon

Shaffir, W. (1999) 'Doing Ethnography', in *Journal of Contemporary Ethnography* 28, 6: 676-86

Shilling, C. (1993) *The Body and Social Theory*, London: Sage

Slater, D. (1997) *Consumer Culture and Modernity*, Cambridge: Polity Press

Smith, D. (1988) *The Chicago School: a Liberal Critique of Capitalism*, Basingstoke: Macmillan Education

Smith, D. (1990) *Texts, Facts, and Femininity: Exploring the Relations of Ruling*, London: Routledge

Smith, S. and Watson, J. (1996) (eds) *Getting a Life: Everyday Uses of Autobiography*, London: University of Minnesota Press

Soja, E. (1989) *Postmodern Geographies: the Reassertion of Space in Critical Social Theory*, London: Verso

Sparks, C. and Tulloch, J. (2000) (eds) *Tabloid Tales: Global Debates Over Media Standards*, New York: Rowan & Littlefield

Spender, D. (1995) *Nattering on the Net: Women, Power and Cyberspace*, Melbourne: Spinifex

Spivak, G. (1990) *The Post-Colonial Critic: Interviews, Strategies, Dialogues*, New York: Routledge

Staiger, R. (1979) *Roads to Reading*, Paris: UNESCO

Steiner, G. (1973) *Do Books Matter?* Leeds: Morley Books

Steiner, G. (1988) 'Literature Today', in *Books in the 1990s: The Proceedings of the 23rd International Publishers Association*, London: Congress Bowker/Saur

Storey, J. (1994) *Cultural Theory and Popular Culture: a Reader*, London: Harvester/ Wheatsheaf

Storey, J. (1997) *An Introduction to Cultural Theory and Popular Culture*, 2nd ed., London: Harvester/Wheatsheaf

Sutherland, G. (1973) (ed) *Arnold on Education*, Harmondsworth: Penguin

Taksa, L. and Lyons, M. (1992) *Australian Readers Remember: An Oral History of Reading 1890-1930*, Melbourne: Oxford University Press

Thomas, J. (1993) *Doing Critical Ethnography*, London: Sage

Thompson, E.P. (1963) *The Making of the English Working Class*, Harmondsworth: Penguin

Thompson, J. (1995) *The Media and Modernity: A Social History of the Media*, Oxford: Polity Press

Thornton, S. (1995) *Club Cultures: Music, Media and Subcultural Capital*, Hanover: Wesleyan University Press and University Press of New England

Thrift, N. (1996) *Spatial Formations*, London: Sage

Tonkin, E. (1992) *Narrating Our Past: The Social Construction of Oral History*, London: Cambridge University Press

Tuan, Y.-F. (1977) *Space and Place: the Perspective of Experience*, Minneapolis: University of Minnesota Press

Turner, G. (1996) *British Cultural Studies: An Introduction*, London: Unwin Hyman

Urry, J. (1995) *Consuming Places*, London: Routledge

Van Maanen, J. (1988) *Tales of the Field*, Chicago: Chicago University Press

Van Maanen, J. (1995) 'An End to Innocence: The Ethnography of Ethnography', in J. Van Maanen (ed) *Representation in Ethnography*, California: Sage

Van Maanen, J. (1995) (ed) *Representation in Ethnography*, California: Sage

Vaughan, S. (1983) 'The Community of the Book', in S. Graubard (ed) *Reading in the 1980s*, New York: Bowker

Vincent, D. (2000) *The Rise of Mass Literacy: Reading and Writing in Modern Europe*, Cambridge: Polity Press

Wark, M. (1999) *Celebrities, Culture and Cyberspace*, Sydney: Pluto Press

Watson, G. (1978) *The Story of the Novel*, London: Macmillan

Watt, I. (1963) *The Rise of the Novel*, Middlesex: Peregrine

Weber, M. (1930) *The Protestant Ethic and the Spirit of Capitalism*, London: Unwin University Books

Weedon, C. (1997) *Feminist Practice and Poststructuralist Theory*, London: Blackwell

Wellman, D. (1994) 'Constituting Ethnographic Authority: The Work Process of Field Research, an Ethnographic Account', in *Cultural Studies* 8, 2: 569:593

Whissen, T.R. (1992) *Classic Cult Fiction: A Companion to Popular Cult Fiction*, New York: Greenwood Press

Williams, R. (1958) *Culture and Society*, London: The Hogarth Press

Williams, R. (1965) *The Long Revolution*, London: Pelican

Williams, R. (1971) *Orwell*, London: Fontana

Williams, R. (1974) *Television: Technology and Cultural Form*, Fontana: London

Williams, R. (1976) *Keywords: A Vocabulary of Culture and Society*, New York: Oxford University Press

Williams, R. (1977) *Marxism and Literature*, London: Oxford University Press

Williams, R. (1981) *Culture*, London: Fontana

Williamson, D. (1989) *Authorship and Criticism*, Sydney: Local Consumption

Willis, P. (1990) *Common Culture: Symbolic Work at Play in the Everyday Cultures of the Young*, Milton Keynes: Open University Press

Willis, P. (1990a) 'Notes on Method', in S. Hall (ed) *Culture, Media, Language*, London: Hutchinson

Willis, P. (2001) *The Ethnographic Imagination*, Cambridge: Polity Press

Willis, P. and Trondmann, M. (2000) 'Manifesto for *Ethnography*', in *Ethnography* 1, 1: 5-16

Willmot, P. (1987) *Friendship Networks and Social Support*, London: Policy Studies Institute

Wilson, M. (1992) 'Asking Questions', in R. Sapsford and V. Jupp (eds) *Data Collection and Analysis*, London: Sage and Open University Press

Wimsatt, W.K. (1970) *The Verbal Icon: Studies in the Meaning of Poetry*, London, Methuen

Windsor, J. (1994) 'Identity Parades', in J. Elsner and R, Cardinal (eds) *The Culture of Collecting*, Melbourne: Melbourne University Press

Wise, J.M. (2000) 'Home: Territory and Identity', in *Cultural Studies* 14, 2: 295-310

Wolcott, H.F. (1995) 'Making a Study "More Ethnographic"', in J. Van Maanen (ed) *Representation in Ethnography*, California: Sage

Wolff, J. (1993) *The Social Production of Art*, Basingstoke: Macmillan

Wood, H. (2004) 'What Reading the Romance Did for Us', in *European Journal of Cultural Studies*, 7, 2: 147-154

Young, S. (2007) *The Book is Dead, Long Live the Book*, Sydney: University of New South Wales Press

Appendix A: Readers' Profiles

Anthony (A)

Anthony is 34 and has just begun a part-time undergraduate degree at a Sydney University. He lives with his girlfriend in a unit in Sydney's east. He was recently made unemployed. His mother has always been a big reader but as far as he can remember his father, who has been employed in a number of blue-collar occupations, 'never read anything'. He attended a state high school in Sydney, but left in Year 11; school was not a happy experience. He continued to read, especially science fiction and fantasy. As an adult, however, his tastes have changed. Anthony now prefers 'classic books' and 'acclaimed' novels: Jane Austen is 'probably' his favourite author. He's uncertain of the number of hours he reads each week and is certain he is a slow reader: he reads one novel about every three weeks. His slow reading and an abundant supply of novels means that he never re-reads because there are 'so many other books to read'. His desire to read as widely as possible is fuelled by a belief that he is not very well read. Over the last few years he has been getting his 'life back on track', so he has not had a lot of spare time. When he does, he likes to write and would like to be a writer in the future. Other than writing he likes to go recreational fishing and watch history and nature documentaries on television.

Belinda (B)

Belinda is 26. She works as a research officer for a university division and rents a flat in Sydney's east. She reads novels for about six hours per week and is a member of the local library. She buys both new and second-hand books, and spends about $20-$30 per month. Despite reading different kinds of books, she is averse to 'heavy literature' and does not like science fiction, or fantasy or detective writing. She cites Michael Ondaatje, John Berendt and non-fiction writer Bill Bryson as particular favourites. She never re-reads books or magazines, but she does read the newspaper. Born and schooled in Tasmania, her mother is a teacher. Belinda holds a social science degree.

Catarina (C)

Catarina is 22 and lives in a unit with a friend in eastern Sydney. She went to a Catholic girls' high school. Last year she completed her undergraduate media degree. Her mother, who works as an English and history teacher, likes to read anything historical, including biographies. Her father is a house-husband who reads non-fiction. Currently, Catarina works in a university library. She also writes part-time for independent music and entertainment publications, including the 'street press'. At the time of the interview, Catarina was not reading as much as normal, which is between eight and ten hours per week. She buys most of her books, but she is also lent quite a few by her friends and her mother. Although varied in her tastes, she does not like science fiction or fantasy literature. Apart from reading recommendations from friends she has no method for choosing books, other than trying to fit the book to her mood. Her last book was Nick Hornby's *High Fidelity*. Catarina often reads more than one novel at once, and believes this is because she gets bored easily. She is also a frequent re-reader. Other than books she also reads a lot of music-related media: magazines, newspapers and on-line sources. She is very interested in music, plays the guitar and has been a member of a number of working bands that have performed around inner Sydney. She sees bands perform live. Her interest in music extends to radio; she listens to Triple-J radio to learn about the 'music scene', which aids her writing.

Dirk (D)

Dirk is 21 and in his last year of an undergraduate university course. He went to a selective boys' high school. He lives at home with his parents, both readers, in a north-west Sydney suburb and works part-time in a bottle-shop. His favourite books and authors are all from the fantasy and science fiction genres—David Eddings, Robert Jordan and Raymond E. Feist are particular favourites. He especially likes novels with 'complex plots'. His least favourite books are those dominated by 'heavy description'. Dirk describes his reading as erratic. Sometimes he'll read three books in a week, on other occasions none at all. During his heavy reading weeks he'll read for five hours per day. He re-reads many of his books because 'there are a lot of words' in those long fantasy series. Of all the readers interviewed Dirk is the only one who could be described as a fan: he attends conventions, book readings and buys books from specialist bookshops as well as usual outlets. His reading does not normally extend to magazines or newspapers. Although he reads a lot he manages to watch some television, but only 'to veg out'. He likes sitcoms like *Friends* and *Seinfeld*, and the animated series *South Park*. Rather than watch television he'll play games including computer, board and card games—he is something of a poker player.

Eric (E)

Although he now rents a flat with his girlfriend in the eastern suburbs, Eric, age 26, attended a state high school in Sydney's western suburbs. His mother is a nurse, his father works in sales management, and both are readers. In fact, his father is a major source of books as he has accumulated a 'serious' library over the years. Eric studied audio engineering at TAFE before enrolling in a media degree at university. He works part-time to support himself. Eric reads novels for about seven hours per week. He especially likes reading science fiction and reads a lot of 'literature': he cites J.R.R. Tolkien and Herman Hesse as his favourite authors. He gets nearly all his books new, often re-reads and also finds time for newspapers and magazines, often music- or film- related, and playing guitar.

Frances (F)

Frances, 27, is employed as the administration manager in a Sydney printing company. She is single and lives with her parents in a house in the city's southern suburbs. She was educated at a state selective school. After completing year 12 she studied speech pathology for a year at university, 'which was horrible'. She later attended TAFE, secretarial and administration management studies, and most recently she completed a desktop publishing course at a private college. Her father, who is a marine mechanic, rarely, if ever, reads fiction, but her mother, who is a purchasing officer for a large retail company, is very keen on novels, which she and Frances often share. She reads for about eight hours per week, mostly while in bed. Other than reading, Frances likes going to hear live music.

Georgina (G)

Georgina, 21, grew up in a 'solid middle-class family'. Both her reading parents are accountants. She attended a selective state 'performing arts' high school before going to university to study for a media degree. She has part-time work in hospitality. Of all the interviewees, Georgina read the least: two hours per week. During holiday periods, however, her reading increases exponentially: she often devours three or four novels per week when she visits her parents who live on the south coast of New South Wales. She thinks that she has a very broad taste in novels, Milan Kundera to John Grisham, but draws a line at crime fiction and Nick Hornby because he's 'too blokey'. Most of the books she really likes are linked through 'good writing'. A frequent reader, she will return to particular passages or chapters that resonate with her. Isabelle Allende is her favourite author: 'she writes beautifully'. Although she is an avid newspaper reader, she does not read magazines, especially women's magazines, which she 'has banned from the house'.

Recently, she has become very interested in non-fiction books about politics and globalisation. Georgina shares a flat with friends in Sydney's east. She has no favourite television programmes at the moment, so her television set is used mainly for watching videos. She feels that she is the only twenty-something woman who does not like *Buffy the Vampire Slayer*.

Ivana (I)

Ivana is 29 and lives with her boyfriend in the 'back of a house' in Sydney's inner-west. She has just started a degree course after completing a university access programme and went to a Catholic girls' high school. She was born in Argentina, but due to the political upheavals in that country she and her family moved first to Spain, and finally to Australia. Her father was an official in the Argentinian labour movement, but since coming to Australia he has worked for a cleaning company. Her mother and father have always been voracious readers of both fiction and non-fiction. Her father will only read books in Spanish. She reads for pleasure for approximately three hours per week. Ivana gets most of her books new or borrows them from her local library. She is a frequent re-reader of books and cites Garcia Marquez and Camus as favourite authors. As she is bilingual she also reads a lot of female Argentinian writers that 'you wouldn't have heard of'. Ivana likes 'to read in Spanish because I'm afraid of losing it, and I am losing it'. She stays well away from romance novels and most science fiction books. She also reads non-fiction: John Pilger's text *Hidden Agenda* is a particular obsession. She generally avoids commercial television stations because they're too 'trashy'. However, she really likes the ABC and SBS, particularly the documentaries and foreign films. Ivana also likes going to the cinema. As well as books, she reads 'trashy magazines' which she borrows from friends. She works in the hospitality industry.

Julie (J)

Julie, at 51, is the oldest of the interviewees. She works as a university administrator. She holds an undergraduate degree in arts and is undertaking a postgraduate qualification part-time. She grew up in rural western Australia and now lives in a mortgaged unit in the eastern suburbs of Sydney with her husband, who is a nurse. She reads for pleasure for about three or four hours per week, much less than she would like. Julie also reads magazines 'and even things like *Readers Digest*'. Her parents were 'both great readers', and she attributes their passion for stories as the catalyst for her interest in fiction. Her current novel is Michael Cunningham's *The Hours*. As well as reading she spends time bush-walking and visiting museums and galleries when she can.

Karen (K)

Karen, 30, was educated at a private secondary school in south-west London. Her father is academic engineer, her mother 'stayed at home', but she also has a higher degree and has worked as a TEFL teacher. Karen has bachelor and masters' degrees in psychology and works as a psychologist in the public sector. Due to the pressure of work she no longer reads classic novels as she once did, preferring now to engage with science fiction, fantasy, detective fiction, thrillers and 'contemporary novels', which she reads for approximately seven hours per week. Despite being broad in her taste, she would never consider reading a 'Mills and Boon' or a 'Bryce Courtney'. Not a magazine reader, she nonetheless endeavours to read the newspaper. She lives with her husband in a rented 'half a house' in Sydney's inner west.

Lana (L)

Lana is a 24-year-old postgraduate student living on a federal government scholarship. She attended a private girls' school and holds a BA/BEd degree. Her father is a barrister, her mother a housewife and both are 'big readers'. She reads a great deal and although she did not know her exact number of hours per week, it is enough to 'polish off um ... a book a week'. She professed to a wide range of novel reading interests: 'cyberpunk novels, I like futuristic novels, [...] at the moment I'm reading Kerry Hume's *The Bone People*, last week I read *Beloved* again, week before that I was reading [*The*] *Hitch-Hiker's Guide to the Galaxy*'. She often re-reads books, buys books new and second-hand and undertakes book-buying binges: 'So I get depressed, most people buy clothes, cars or mobile phones or ... things for the garden when they're depressed but I go and buy seven or eight books and have a bill of $150 out of my account.' She also likes reading food magazines and is a fan of television science fiction and fantasy series like *Star Trek*, *The X-Files* and *Buffy the Vampire Slayer*. She is currently renting a two-bedroom flat in Sydney's east.

Madelaine (M)

Madelaine, aged 49, grew-up in New Zealand and did not have a TV until she was thirteen: 'reading was the only recreation'. She went to technical college in New Zealand until she was 14. She has worked as a librarian for a number of years and has continued her education part-time: 'Library Science undergraduate degree, [...] distance learning, eight years! Adult Education Graduate Diploma, [...] part-time 2 years, MEd. [...] part-time 3 years'. She reads 'all sorts' of books except '... Stephen King-type stuff' and reads every day: 'I like lots of authors but if I had to choose, Jeanette Winterson, Michael Ondaatje, Salman Rushdie, Faye Weldon, Tim Powers, Umberto Eco,

Margaret Atwood, Tolkien'. She buys most of her books, new and second-hand, spending about $50 a month. A third of her books come from friends and the library. She finds about ten hours per week in which to read for pleasure. She sometimes reads magazines, especially 'those recipe food magazines you can buy in supermarkets'. When she's not reading, Madelaine likes gardening, some handicrafts, 'I do mosaics, very slowly, I have been doing the laundry wall for years!', visiting art galleries, walking, watching films and spending time with her grown-up family. She lives with her husband.

Natasha (N)

Natasha's mother and father are both teachers who value fiction reading. Her parents' progressive attitude to education resulted in her attendance at a Rudolph Steiner school from Kindergarten until Year 12. Natasha is currently enrolled in an arts and social science degree programme at a Sydney university and works part-time for the New South Wales Department of Community Services. She likes 'semi-historical' novels, especially the work of Michael Ondaatjee. On average she manages to read for about two hours per day, but this expands during holiday periods. As there are so many books on offer she never feels like re-reading. As well as reading, she spends time bush-walking and going to the cinema. Although she does not have an interest in magazines she will read the newspaper, especially at the weekend. Natasha rents a flat with her boyfriend in the eastern suburbs. She is 21 years of age.

Roz (R)

Roz's father, now retired, was an electrical engineer in the public sector, while her mother, also retired, worked in retail. She was educated in a mixture of private and public schools, and went on to complete an arts degree in 1996. She is 26 years old. After finishing university she completed a desktop publishing diploma at a private college. She now works as a graphic designer for a small niche-market publisher. In terms of volume, Roz is the biggest reader interviewed: she reads for about 21 hours per week. She reads lots of different books but particularly likes magic-realism, science fiction and classics, while her favoured authors include Gabriel Garcia Marquez, Angela Carter, Jonathon Kellerman and Clive Barker. Despite re-reading a lot, Roz still spends about $50 per month on books, both new and second-hand. She also reads magazines but not newspapers and not women's magazines, 'which bore me stupid because I don't give a toss about my hair or my make-up for one thing, and you know, getting laid, having massive orgasms, doesn't strike me as the focus of my life'. She lives in a rented flat with a friend in one of Sydney's eastern suburbs.

Susan (S)

Susan's mother and father—who works in banking—are both big readers. Susan, 31, reads for about 14 hours per week. She re-reads books, and tries to buy second-hand titles if she can. She also watches a fair amount of television, including the soap opera *Neighbours*. Although she does not buy them, Susan reads magazines like *Who Weekly* and *New Weekly*. Her favourite author is William Faulkner. She has 'never really gotten into science fiction' because 'I like things to be a bit real'. Susan attended a private boarding school and holds a BA (Hons) and postgraduate qualifications. She works as an English teacher at a private high school and lives with her husband and daughter in Sydney's inner west.

Terri (T)

Terri is 39 years old and works as a publications officer and desktop publisher in the public sector. She attended a public girls' high school and is currently attending university part-time. Terri is married (to a painter) and lives in a rented unit in a beach-side Sydney suburb. Her parents were both stage entertainers before they retired. Terri is very broad in her choice of reading, but would not read Mills and Boon, Robert Ludlum or 'anything with guns on the cover or names like Bolt or Colt because I'm not their audience, they are not meant for me in my opinion'. She quite likes to re-read books and has been known to read a particularly enjoyable book twice in quick succession. Terri buys books new and second-hand, from shops, markets and garage sales. Although she does not really know how many hours she reads a week, Terri estimates that 20 hours a week is close. As well as reading, Terri finds time for yoga, walking on the beach, going to pubs, film and theatre.

Vincent (V)

Vincent is a 42-year-old gay man who rents a house in a central suburb of Sydney. Despite the huge amount of professional reading he is required to undertake for his teaching at a Sydney university, he still manages two hours' recreational reading per day. His 'reading for pleasure' occurs mostly in bed and he often reads in Spanish. He reads widely but prefers not to read texts that are too overtly heterosexual. Vincent grew up in Canberra, attended a public high school and studied at tertiary level for 14 years: he holds first degrees in arts and visual arts. He also has a PhD. His parents were both police officers before retirement. Vincent manages to fit about thirty hours of television into an average week. He has eclectic tastes in programmes: he likes the crime series *Inspector Rex*, wildlife documentaries ('they have appealing narratives') and is 'addicted' to the reality-TV show *Popstars*.

Winston (W)

Winston is a 25-year-old postgraduate student at a Sydney university. He supplements his scholarship with work as a part-time high school English tutor. His father is a pharmacist, his mother a teacher's aid. He attended a private co-ed high school and holds a BA (Hons). He lives in a rented unit in the inner-western suburbs of Sydney. Winston told me that he was as a 'bit of an elitist' when it comes to books: 'I'm very much a bit of a snob'. For this reason he tends not to read bestsellers. Despite the fact that his studies impinge upon his leisure reading, he manages nonetheless to read for between three and six hours per week, which equates to about three or four novels a month. This lack of time makes re-reading an uncommon activity because 'there is just too much out there'. Although not a magazine reader, he does read the newspaper. His books come from a number of sources: friends, libraries and second-hand bookshops. As well as reading, his leisure activities include cinema, especially 'art-house' films, and playing the guitar 'a bit'. He chooses not to watch much television, but when he does he prefers documentaries and *Buffy the Vampire Slayer*.

Yvonne (Y)

Yvonne is a 22-year-old student who lives in a unit in a south-eastern Sydney suburb. She was born in Hong Kong but has also lived in America, Taiwan and Australia. Her father is a university lecturer and her mother is a housewife. She went to a number of different private schools and is bilingual; she speaks both English and Cantonese. Yvonne normally reads one or two novels a week (or for about five hours), but when on holidays she may read as many as three. She likes 'easy-reading contemporary fiction' with realistic storylines because 'I don't like to think or imagine too much'. She doesn't read science fiction, it is 'too far off'. She re-reads lots of books to 'get the bits you didn't get the first time'. She is a member of her local library, but still manages to buy more books than she borrows. She will often choose to read a novel because she 'likes the cover'. Other than books, she reads a few magazines, like *Who Weekly* (to which she has a subscription), but never bothers with the newspaper. She watches about three hours of television a night and will often read a book while doing so. She works part-time in an Asian supermarket.

Zoe (Z)

Zoe is a 22-year-old medical student. She supports herself financially through two part-time retail jobs. Zoe grew up in a one-parent family in Brisbane where she attended a private girls' high school. Describing herself as a 'book-person', she especially likes reading because it is 'a way of experiencing the world without paying much money'. Her mother, who always encouraged her to read as a child, is currently 'doing a PhD' part-time. Zoe reads novels, most of which she gets second-hand, for about six hours per week. She reads all sorts of books but not horror, Stephen King, or Mills and Boon. She has recently started reading science fiction again after 'forgetting' the genre for a few years. She had just read Neal Stephenson's *Cryptonomicon* and Toni Morrison's *Paradise*. In addition to novel reading, she also reads *HQ* magazine and *Cleo*, and will read Saturday's newspapers. She does watch some television, especially *ER*, a medical drama that is compulsory viewing for her medical student friends. Other than reading, she likes to go to the gym and 'drink red wine'. She lives in a rented unit in the eastern suburbs with a friend who is also a 'big reader'.

Appendix B: Conducting the Interviews

The interviews began with questions about reading histories and reading in general, followed by demographic questions and, finally, a discussion of a particular novel. Unlike studies based on prolonged and frequent contact between researchers and subjects, interview-based work does not allow as much time for the building of a rapport between participants; the way in which the interview is conducted is therefore highly important because 'the relationship between the knower and the known substantially shapes the findings' (Ganguly-Scrase 1998:44). It came as no surprise to find that the interviews in which little rapport was established between myself and the interviewee produced the least useable transcripts. In an effort to make the readers feel at ease the demographic questions, often the mostly highly sensitive questions asked in an interview situation, were located in the middle of the interview. This was because personal questions asked at the beginning of an interview may be regarded as impolite, whereas those asked at the interview's conclusion may appear like a disinterested afterthought.

After considering the possible effects of the intended place of interview on audience participation (Seiter 1999:32), the readers were interviewed in a location of their choice: at home, at work, in a local park, cafe or hotel. This was not designed to replicate the conditions in which their reading performances occurred, although some do read in these places, but to afford the interviewees a feeling of control over the interview process, albeit a limited one. My exchanges with the readers were recorded for subsequent transcription. On some occasions the discussions continued after the tape-recorder was switched-off. In these instances I took notes manually.

Below is a list of the subject areas addressed during the interviews conducted for this book. This list does not encapsulate everything that was discussed during the hours of conversations that form the basis of this research. Even though some of these questions were posed to solicit specific information about reading, readers often treated all questions as catalysts for a much wider debate. Readers often took the discussion into unexpected territory.

General question areas

Reading History

early reading experience	parental reading habits and influence
reading for school	library use
childhood attitude toward books	

Novel Reading

numbers of books read	when and where
reading time	preferences for specific genres or authors
'good' and 'bad' books	re-reading texts
reading pleasure	influences on reading
book storage	why read?

Acquiring Books

sourcing books	buying books: new or second-hand
book discussions	library borrowing
borrowing/lending	

Other Reading

other printed material	books compared with other media
non-fiction	magazines and newspapers
other leisure activities	on-line resources

Demographic questions

age	sex
relationship status	occupation
income	education
accommodation	language spoken in the home
ethnic origin	religious preference

Beloved question areas

source of novel	when and where read
knowledge of author	knowledge of the text
expectations	the book's qualities/features/attributes
likes and dislikes	other Morrison novels? How did it compare?
difficulty?	generic comparisons
intertextual comparisons	comparisons with the film

Index